Railway Design since 1830

Volume 1: 1830–1914

Brian Haresnape

Railway Design since 1830

Volume 1
1830–1914

LONDON
IAN ALLAN

For Claire

© Brian Haresnape 1968.

Published by
IAN ALLAN LTD,
SHEPPERTON, SURREY.

Set in 9 on 11 Univers,
& printed in Great Britain by
R. J. Acford Ltd.,
Chichester, Sussex.

7110 0029 8

Contents

Acknowledgements

The Author would like to express his gratitude to the following for their advice and assistance in the preparation of volume one of this work: Alec Swain, J. E. Kite, G. M. Kichenside and V. K. Welch.

For assistance in obtaining illustrations, the following owners and photographers are warmly thanked:

H. C. Casserley, figure 191; C. R. L. Coles, figures 153, 188; J. Cupit, figure 233; Greenwich Libraries, figure 238; G. F. Heiron, figure 168; Photomatic Ltd., figure 210; Alec Swain, figures 229, 230, 232; S. C. Townroe, figure 203. The following collections are also sincerely thanked for the loan of material which is reproduced by their courtesy: Curator of Historical Relics, British Railways Board, *frontispiece* and figures 18, 27, 31, 36, 41, 42, 51, 55, 67, 77, 79, 88, 105, 106, 113, 119, 121, 124, 135, 139, 145, 165, 183, 187, 194, 198, 199, 204, 205, 207, 212, 218, 219, 223, 225, 228, 231, 234, 235. British Railways, Eastern Region, figures 12, 34, 35, 47, 56, 60, 69, 71, 151, 156, 157, 161, 162, 169, 170, 171, 174, 185, 186, 193, 195, 222. British Railways, London Midland Region, figures 8, 13, 15, 23, 26, 30, 37, 38, 43, 44, 45, 46, 50, 53, 61, 62, 63, 72, 73, 76, 83, 104, 122, 133, 136, 137, 138, 142, 144, 146, 147, 148, 149, 150, 154, 155, 158, 159, 160, 163, 173, 178, 182, 184, 190, 196, 200, 215, 221, 224, 226, 236, 237, 239. British Railways, Southern Region, figures 39, 48, 57, 70, 110, 192. British Railways, Western Region, figures 19, 64, 65, 74, 78, 80, 127, 140, 141, 152, 166, 206, 208, 211, 220. Locomotive Publishing Company, figures 1, 2, 3, 4, 6, 17, 21, 25, 28, 29, 32, 33, 58, 59, 85, 86, 87, 89, 90, 92, 93, 94, 95, 96, 97, 98, 99, 100, 101, 102, 103, 111, 112, 114, 115, 116, 118, 120, 123, 125, 128, 130, 131, 132, 179, 213, 214. Modern Transport, figures 24, 84, 143, 228. Science Museum, figures 5, 7, 9, 11, 20, 22, 40, 75.

The following figures are from the Author's personal collection: 10, 16, 49, 52, 54, 66, 68, 81, 82, 91, 107, 108, 109, 117, 126, 129, 134, 164, 167, 176, 177, 197, 201, 202, 209, 216, 217. Figures 172, 175, 180 and 189 are from original drawings by the Author. Figure 181 is from original drawings by V. K. Welch and G. M. Kichenside. Diana Varnon supplied reference for the drawings of decorative station roof valances.

Every care has been taken to credit the illustrations used and no responsibility can be held for any error or omission.

The author also wishes to thank the Chief Public Relations Officer, the Press Officer and the Regional Public Relations and Press Officers, of British Railways, for their untiring efforts on his behalf. Last, but by no means least, his sincere thanks to John Scholes, Curator of Historical Relics British Railways Board, and his assistant Mr. Spence.

Preface to Volume One

The British steam railway might well be described as our greatest gift to the world. It changed the whole face of nations and made immeasurable change to social conditions. The steam locomotive, which made the whole thing possible, has now reached the last years of its useful existence and by 1980 it will probably be extinct, except as an historic item lovingly preserved.

In the period covered in this volume the steam locomotive was developed from a crude invention of uncertain future to a magnificent and highly sophisticated machine, and the later years (from 1870) can truly be described as the ' Golden Age of Steam '.

This is a book about the more abstract qualities, of aesthetics and amenity; about design in the *artistic* sense of the term rather than the technical. It is not intended to be a history in the true sense, although for convenience sake it follows a reasonable chronological order. There are countless books already, on technical and historical development of our railways (enough to fill a small library, in fact). Authors more able than I, have delved deeply into the mechanical operation, into the day-to-day performance, and into the management of the railways of Britain. In passing some have dwelt upon the subject of the appearance of the locomotives, trains and stations. None, to my knowledge, has gone very deeply into the subject (with the notable exception of C. Hamilton Ellis).

This then is a book about the *visual* aspect of railways—or rather I should say, *appeal* of railways. Whether we realise it or not, it is the outward appearance of trains and stations which go to create the individual character. What made the Great Western so different from the London Brighton and South Coast Railway?—Practically every visible item, which was ' stamped ' with the character of the company. As we shall see, this was to a large extent due to the influence of the superb engineers, who paid close attention to the appearance of everything they were associated with.

Locomotives alone do not make the character of a railway, although they are undeniably the ' figurehead ', so to speak. The carriages, stations, liveries, uniforms, signs and notices all contribute towards the general scene.

In dealing with this subject I have deliberately omitted some aspects of our railways. No mention will be found of track or signal design, or of associated railway enterprises such as steamships. I have not discussed goods wagon design (such as it was!), but rather have I deliberately concentrated upon the passenger side of railways. It is this aspect that we all experience, and because it is bound-up so much with our environment as human-beings it is of the greatest importance in our assessment of the character of railways.

By the last years of Queen Victoria's long reign, the British railway companies had established themselves as a virtually monopolistic land transport concern, and they had achieved tremendous progress in the design of locomotives and carriages. What I hope will become apparent to the reader, is that these trains were works of art of a very high order indeed. The locomotives of men like Stroudley, Johnson, Robinson, Wainwright, Dean, and many others, were probably the finest examples of industrial design produced during their period *anywhere in the world*.

Some readers will be surprised to find no interiors of royal carriages discussed or illustrated. Again, the omission is deliberate. These magnificent carriages have been so widely illustrated and described that further repetition seems unnecessary. Some wonderful examples have been preserved at the Museum of British Transport, and anyone can inspect these at will. I have preferred to concentrate upon the day-to-day passenger carriage for my examples of design. Nevertheless it is essential to recognise the fact that the 'Royals' were invariably the most superb examples of coachbuilding, and ahead of their times in terms of amenities.

Many of the illustrations included in the early part of the volume are taken from originals dating back over the last 130 years. Without the masterly draughtsmanship of the topographical artist J. C. Bourne, our record of the early days of the London and Birmingham and the Great Western Railway would be far less complete. Later, the development of reliable portable cameras allowed photographic records of the railway scene to be made. Railway photography has never been an easy proposition, in Victorian days it must have been formidable; with cumbersome equipment and fragile glass negatives. Despite this some superb photographs were obtained, and to all those intrepid enthusiasts of the Victorian era, my sincere thanks for making this volume possible.

Brian Haresnape,
Sussex.
January 1968.

Part One: 1830–1870 The Formative Years

1 | Steam Locomotion Takes Shape

The employment of steam power as a practical alternative to the horse for transporting people and goods, once having been realised, remained to be proven. If the various early solutions *looked* crude it was because that was quite honestly what they were. A great deal of improvisation was to be expected, for both raw materials and machinery were scarcely of the finest quality, and they all too often dictated the limits of inventiveness. As an inevitable result, the early locomotives suffered from many failures and shortcomings, with consequent effects upon their reputation. Thus it is hardly surprising to learn that for some considerable time people's faith in the future of steam locomotion was at a very low ebb indeed.

In his scholarly ' Centennial History of the Liverpool and Manchester Railway ' Dendy Marshall lists only 18 locomotives doing useful work in England in 1825, out of a total of 30 built at various times, and he points out the significant fact that no-one except George Stephenson had continued to build steam locomotives after 1814. A contributory factor to the poor reputation the steam locomotive had gained was the inadequate track, which was far too weak to carry the locomotive's weight and constantly broke under the strain. Fortunately there were others who shared Stephenson's faith in the future of steam railways, but for some time the opposition was sufficiently strong for the whole issue to be very much in the balance. One alternative proposition, with some powerful supporters, envisaged cable haulage driven by stationary winding engines. This system was proposed at one stage in the planning of the Liverpool and Manchester Railway, but in the event George Stephenson and his supporters won the day. However, cable haulage was used on the steeply inclined sections (with stationary steam engines supplied by Robert Stephenson), as the ability of locomotives to haul trains up severe gradients was still seriously questioned.

To the public eye the early locomotives must have looked both ridiculously clumsy and terrifyingly strong. They likened them to horses —but then how else could they judge them? The horse, well trusted and well used (and abused) was an integral part of their everyday environment, in much the same way that the soul-less motor car has become part of ours today. So when the new-fangled steam locomotive made an appearance, before eyes as yet unaccustomed to mechanical invention, and began to perform duties previously entrusted to the horse, the inevitable comparison was drawn. It possessed a crude but strangely lifelike personality. It breathed steam and sighed deeply, or panted. It devoured water and coals with voracious appetite. Soon the inevitable title ' iron horse ' was bestowed upon the brute creation, but only a few visionaries looked to the day when it would replace the horse as the fastest means of travel available to man on earth.

It is interesting to learn that, by 1828, Robert Stephenson was feeling concern over the *appearance* of his locomotives. In a letter to Michael Longridge, one of his partners in the firm, dated January 1st,

1. Steam locomotion had taken crude shape by 1813. This end view of William Hedley's *Puffing Billy* clearly shows the rough manufacture of early locomotives.

2. *Wylam Dilly,* a Hedley locomotive built in 1813 for Wylam Colliery. Seen here in final condition, as running *circa* 1860.

1828, he stated that he had been talking to his father about ' endeavouring to reduce the size and ugliness of our travelling engines '. This he proposed to do by placing the cylinders either on the sides of the boiler or else below it entirely. Timothy Hackworth had in all probability inspired this by the improvements he had demonstrated in his *Royal George* for the Stockton and Darlington Railway, which had proved to be a considerable advance over the two original Stephenson engines built for the line. Robert Stephenson commenced his endeavours with the *Lancashire Witch* of 1829, by placing the cylinders in an inclined position on the side of the boiler, at the rear end, but as yet there were little or no signs of any other improvements in appearance.

Considerably more refined, in proportion and detailing, was his *Rocket* of 1829, a locomotive destined to achieve unparalleled fame. The *Rocket* displayed many signs of Stephenson's efforts to improve the appearance of his designs. The standard of workmanship was much higher than previously existed, and the colour scheme of bright yellow and black, with a white chimney and polished brass mountings, was Stephenson's own choice. The tender is interesting, although very primitive to our eyes it was much better than had until then existed. A well-known coachbuilder, Nathaniel Worsdell, was employed on this The use of a barrel was very much a functional means of carrying the water in a tender constructed mainly of wood.

The story of the Rainhill Trials has been repeated often and well, and does not require further repetition here. It will suffice to say that it established renewed public interest in the iron horse, and demonstrated the suitability beyond question of steam locomotion for the new Liverpool and Manchester Railway. More important still, to our story, it began to show that railways had a certain appeal, as yet latent, of their own. By emerging the winner of the trials Stephenson's *Rocket* helped to set the seal for the future lines of steam locomotive design development in this country. The simple, but rugged and reliable Stephenson

conception was to remain the hallmark of steam locomotives throughout the ensuing century or more.

The *Rocket*, as built, had no smokebox, an external firebox, and steeply inclined cylinders. It was soon rebuilt, with a more dignified chimney mounted upon a proper smokebox. In place of the original tender, a new design with flared raves, and minus the barrel, was attached. The final form had the cylinders lowered to a nearly horizontal position to improve the steadiness of the locomotive when running at speed. A view of this rebuilt design, included in the illustration on page 54, is the only known contemporary one.

After only a few 'improved' *Rocket* (or *Northumbrian*) type locomotives had been constructed, Robert Stephenson introduced his *Planet* type in which (as foreshadowed in his letter to Longridge, already mentioned) he placed the cylinders *inside* and at the front end, and he developed the sandwich frame, of wood between two iron plates—an arrangement which was to be used for more than 50 years, on countless hundreds of locomotives.

Public enthusiasm for the Liverpool and Manchester Railway had exceeded expectations to a degree which caused some astonishment to the directors, who had envisaged the line as chiefly transporting merchandise. One wonders to what degree the elegant little steam engines of Robert Stephenson had helped to convert popular opinion. Certainly by the time he introduced his *Planet*, in 1830, he had transformed the iron horse from a clumsy foot-sore carthorse, to a flighty little thoroughbred which displayed a nice turn of speed. The 'personality' bestowed to each by choice of names, such as *Rocket, Planet, Arrow, Meteor, Dart, Phoenix, Majestic, Mercury, Samson, Goliath* and *Venus*, leaves us in little doubt of the spirit of the times.

Somewhat naturally, the encouraging results of the steam locomotives on the Liverpool and Manchester Railway turned other people's minds towards the lucrative possibilities of locomotive building. Some

3. Stockton and Darlington Railway No. 9 *Middlesbro,* a Timothy Hackworth type locomotive. Note the steeply inclined cylinders and makeshift design of tender.

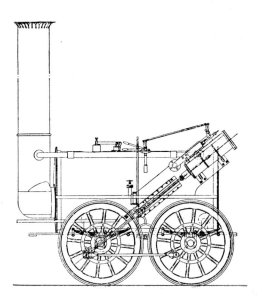

4, *above. Lancashire Witch.* Stephenson's first attempt to 'reduce the ugliness of our travelling engines', showed some Hackworth influence. However his celebrated *Rocket,* **5,** *right,* was a considerable advance in terms of detail design and finish. Illustrated is a scale model showing the original 1829 condition, but unpainted.

weird and wonderful creations were offered to the directors for trials against Stephenson's engines, but the latter remained supreme for the present, in their fitness for purpose and general performance. Two other engineers, Hackworth and Bury, were producing locomotives of a more or less successful nature, but in Hackworth's case they continued to feature what was, by then, a very old fashioned appearance with cylinders steeply inclined, or vertical. In his 0–4–0 engine *Liverpool* of 1830, Edward Bury produced a compact and neat little design with inside cylinders, bar frames, and a 'haystack' firebox (a design which was to be associated with his name for the next quarter of a century). His *Liverpool* was attractive to the eye, and had a most ornate chimney top featuring a design motif of 'liver' birds.

Robert Stephenson & Co. steadily developed the inside cylinder single-driver locomotive, and in their *Patentee* of 1834, we see the precursor of the characteristic British 2–2–2 express passenger locomotive, with sandwich frames. The *Patentee* was basically a lengthened *Planet* with a rear pair of carrying wheels added in an attempt to improve the far from satisfactory riding qualities that were currently being experienced on existing engines. Judged from the aesthetic viewpoint the *Patentee* was a remarkable advance upon the *Rocket* in the short space of five years, and displayed in embryonic form the 'hallmarks' of classic Victorian steam locomotive design. Engine and tender seem to 'belong' and the general sense of balance in the proportions is spoilt only by the rather clumsy chimney, which gives a heavy appearance to the leading end. The driver and fireman are completely exposed to the elements, but at last they have a sensible platform (or footplate) to stand upon, protected at the sides by railings.

Although many strange inventions were still to be vied against the Stephenson conception from time to time, other locomotive builders were quietly beginning to follow his example. As in all trades, men exchanged jobs in search of promotion and better living conditions, and inevitably they took with them a good deal of 'know-how' from previous firms; in such a manner is invention cross-fertilised. Locomotive development proceeded apace, matched by a virtual bonanza of railway building and speculation, and the machinery and manufacturing techniques were also improving steadily. A steady flow of orders for new locomotives encouraged both engineers and builders to yet further improvements in design.

One man who pursued a lone course in locomotive design, persistently remaining faithful to his own ideals, was Edward Bury. He continued to introduce locomotives of his small bar-framed design for service on the London and Birmingham Railway until 1846, by which time they were hopelessly outclassed and undersized, causing considerable embarrassment to that main line.

By the middle 'thirties attention had begun to shift from the industrial North of England where railways were flourishing, to the West, where Brunel's Great Western Railway was to be constructed to a 7ft ' broad gauge '. Stephenson had, until now, settled upon a gauge of 4ft 8½in as suitable for railways, although there were isolated examples which did not conform to this. But 7ft was really courageous and, it seems, quite typical of Brunel's vision. Many historians have lamented the ' battle of the gauges ' which followed in due course, the outcome of which remains with us in the restricted loading gauge of our present railway system. Had Brunel's ideas won the day, what a different course railway history might have followed. But in 1838 no-one could foresee the trouble Brunel's innovation would cause him in the way of opposition, and perhaps this was of scant concern to him, even as a possibility.

For the opening, in 1838, Brunel ordered 20 locomotives, from various manufacturers. Regrettably they proved, when delivered, to be (to quote Ahrons) ' the most extraordinary collection of freaks '. Only two, built by Stephenson, and originally intended for an American 5ft 6in gauge railway, but converted to the 7ft gauge, proved successful. These were the *North Star* and *Morning Star*, and followed Stephenson's typical layout, with sandwich frames and inside cylinders, but being of course somewhat larger than most of his designs. Comparison of the drawings of *North Star* and the *Patentee* shows the family resemblance very well indeed.

At the time of ordering the 20 locomotives Brunel had specified that they should be not only big and fast but as handsome as could be made—because, as he put it, ' a plain young lady, however amiable, is apt to be neglected '. Evidently Stephenson's attempts to produce good-looking locomotives were enthusiastically received by Brunel, for when awaiting delivery of the two locomotives, he wrote to Stephenson stating ' I look forward to having such an engine as never before '. When he actually received *North Star* he became so excited by it that he wrote to a friend ' We have a splendid engine of Stephenson's, it would have been a beautiful ornament in the most elegant drawing room '.

We might pause here, on this enthusiastic note, and briefly

6. Stephenson's 'PLANET' class of 1830 for the Liverpool and Manchester Railway. The cylinders were placed under the boiler and between the sandwich frames. The overall design had a neat simplicity which was to become characteristic of Stephenson's engines.

7. The pretty little *Novelty* was destined to remain exactly what its name implied. Nevertheless it was a favourite amongst the spectators at the Rainhill Trials. This delightful drawing by the engineer Charles Vignoles gives a very good idea of the small dimensions of the locomotive.

consider the stylistic trends of the British steam locomotive, as they were evolving in the years 1838–1840. We have noted the way in which Stephenson's *Patentee* foreshadowed the shape of things to come; whilst one or two engineers produced quite successful alternative conventions. The typical passenger engine was of Stephenson inspiration, with inside cylinders, sandwich frames and neat clean lines. Boilers generally had a clothing of wooden (mahogany) lagging strips, which were tenoned and grooved, and then finished by staining and varnishing, or perhaps paint and varnish. As a rule, boiler bands of polished brass, or painted metal, were bound around the wooden clothing. The exterior of the firebox had been left bare until now, with rivet heads showing, but it was becoming the practice to lag these with wood, at least partially. The actual shape of the firebox ranged from the slightly raised round topped variety (as on *Patentee*), to the distinctive 'haystacks' of Edward Bury which were D-shaped and made first in iron and later copper, and to the equally distinctive 'Gothic' firebox, so called because it had a somewhat pointed pyramidal shape to the top of the casing. Chimney design had changed considerably over the 10 years since *Rocket* had sported its spike-topped affair and Bury's *Liverpool* had had 'liver' birds grouped around the rim. The typical chimney was now a cylindrical iron casing of considerable height, with parallel sides and built-up in two or three sections. The top was flared like a bellmouth, and possibly of polished metal. Boiler mountings were beginning to display a certain elegance of their own, with polished brass or copper finish. No protection was given to the enginemen apart from handrails each side, and no doubt they welcomed the high 'haystack' or 'Gothic' fireboxes for the added shelter they afforded!

By now, other builders were establishing their own typical appearance-design, just as Stephenson had done, and the next 10 years were to see considerable invention in applied ornament for locomotives, with the products of different makers being readily identifiable by the style of boiler mountings and other details.

As already mentioned, apart from *North Star* and her sister engine, the remaining 18 locomotives ordered by Brunel for the GWR did not come up to expectations. Faced with the problem of building a stud of reliable new engines to operate the line, Daniel Gooch, the young man appointed in charge of the Locomotive Department (in his early twenties), took Stephenson's design as the basis for his own *Firefly* class 2–2–2's, of which 62 were built to a standard specification by various firms between 1840–42. At the time these were without equal in terms of power and speed. No doubt the disastrous experience of the initial batch of 20 locomotives Brunel had ordered helped Gooch to establish a case for standardisation, and he issued full specifications and templates to each builder to ensure this!

By one of those curious twists of fate, Robert Stephenson, having established the successful basis of the nineteenth century steam locomotive, then proceeded to lose sight of it for a while by trying to establish the 'long-boiler' design. He was anxious to obtain a lower centre of gravity, and also to increase boiler efficiency, and set out to do this by designing a long, low boiler. But the turntables in current use restricted him to a short wheelbase, with the result that the wheels were all crammed into the space between the back of the smokebox and the front of the firebox, with a considerable overhang each end. Except for freight duties, they were not a great success, proving unsteady at speed; nevertheless large numbers of 'long-boiler' engines were produced up to 1847. However, on the Continent 'long-boiler' engines proved more successful.

Another attempt to lower the centre of gravity was that of T. R. Crampton, who conceived the idea of putting the single driving wheels right behind the boiler and firebox. This meant that only small diameter carrying wheels need be placed below the boiler, which could therefore be pitched lower than was possible when allowance had to be made for the driving axle. Crampton's engines had a very mixed reception in this country, with more than their share of troubles, but the basic idea was a brilliant one, and, like Stephenson's 'long-boilers', on the Continent they were far more successful, for some obscure reason. Anyhow a 'Crampton' was a most distinguished locomotive to gaze upon, with the huge driving wheel set right back with the enginemen placed on a footplate within two commodious splashers. The photograph of *Kinnaird,* of the Dundee, Perth and Aberdeen Junction Railway, reproduced on page 20 very strikingly portrays the individual character of a Crampton engine. Particularly noteworthy is the use of external valve gear to the driving wheel at a time when most designers were following Stephenson's example and hiding this discreetly from view. Perhaps the 'Cramptons' were too foreign to the English eye to be readily accepted; certainly they possessed a totally different aesthetic quality to most of their contemporaries.

Whilst Stephenson and Crampton had been involved in their experiments, just described, other locomotive builders were steadily producing their own progressively improved variants of Stephenson's *Patentee.* Notable were the *Sharpies* of Sharp, Roberts and Company, built as their standard railway engine for many different companies, and perhaps most famous of all the *Jenny Lind* design by David Joy for E. B. Wilson. This is usually held up as the finest example of the designs of the period, in aesthetic terms, and study of the drawing tends to

8. A typical Edward Bury locomotive of the London and Birmingham Railway, with 'haystack' firebox, inside cylinders and bar frames. No. 32, a 2-2-0, is shown leaving the Camden Town engine house in this detail from a lithograph by J. C. Bourne. 9, *below,* Stephenson's inside cylinder 2-2-2 standard passenger engine of 1838, a later example of the *Patentee* of 1834.

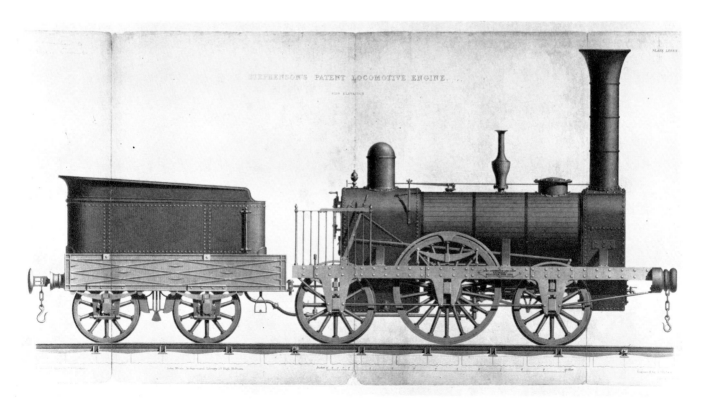

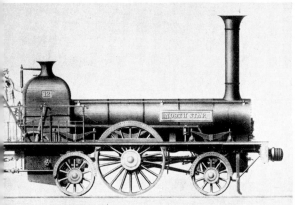

This page:

10, *above left*. *North Star,* a Stephenson long-boiler design for the Northern and Eastern Railway, 1841. (This railway ran between London and Bishops Stortford, and was 5ft. guage.) Note the size of the boiler compared to the man. Another Stephenson engine named *North Star,* is far better known. This locomotive, **11,** *above right,* and the similar *Morning Star* were delivered to the 7ft. gauge Great Western Railway. Brunel was most enthusiastic about them, and alone of the initial twenty locomotives ordered for the line they were to prove successful in service.

Opposite page:

12, *top*. A Sharp Brothers 'SHARPIE' of 1843. A Stephenson derivative, with sandwich frames and inside cylinders. Noteworthy are the side-sheets to the footplate, the metal boiler casing, and the impressive dome. Both chimney and dome have square bases.

13, *bottom*. A later Stephenson long-boiler design, for the London and North Western Railway, 1847.

confirm this widely held opinion. There is an undeniable grace about the whole design, whilst handling of the details is nowhere clumsy. The fluted dome and safety valve columns lend a distinctly classical air to these dominant features, whilst the chimney has more slender and dainty proportions than hitherto. The inside bearings used for the driving axle, together with the slotted treatment of the splasher give the big wheel an elegant appearance. Points of interest are the square bases to both dome and safety valve (see photographs on page 19) and the metal sidesheets now enclosing the handrails on the footplate sides and extending round to meet the side of the firebox.

The use of distinctive detail design, for example the fluted treatment of dome and safety valve with hemispherical cover to the dome mounted upon a square base (shown on *Jenny Lind*), became (as remarked earlier) a form of trademark adopted by builders to distinguish their products. Some chose very simple but shapely treatments, others went in for elaborate and imposing affairs, more suited to architecture than engineering (note the dome casing shown on Crampton's *Kinnaird*, page 20). Perhaps the choicest of all was that adopted by R. & W. Hawthorn, and illustrated on pages 18 and 26. This was of plain flared iron, but beautifully matched for chimney, dome and safety valve casings. The drawing of *Plews* (page 18) shows how well this scheme fitted the overall appearance.

This marriage of aesthetics and engineering was partly instinctive but, as we have seen, partly deliberate. A developing sense of fitness for purpose is evident in such lovely designs as the *Jenny Lind*; just as the most beautiful sailing ships evolved from crude beginnings, so the steam locomotive progressed—but in a very short time indeed. No longer did crudity of manufacture make itself apparent in the finished product, the outward aspect was one of great attention to detail. This is one of the most fascinating aspects of locomotive design during the period 1830–1851, namely that it stood almost alone as an example of true machine produced design, developing naturally out of constant search for improvement and refinement, and assuming shape through this process.

One final locomotive type produced prior to 1851 remains to be mentioned, namely Alexander Allan's *Crewe Type*. This was clearly distinguished by having outside cylinders, slightly inclined, supported on double frames with a flowing curve linking smokebox wrapper and cylinders, and continuing under the cylinders to meet the outside frame.

PASSENGER ENGINE

SHEFFIELD & MANCHESTER RAILWAY

SHARP BROTHERS & Co

MANCHESTER 1845

STEPHENSON'S PATENT LOCOMOTIVE ENGINE.

SCALE OF FEET

The leading and trailing wheels were supported on outside bearings and the driving wheel on inside bearings. The side rods were between the frames which had a slot cut into them to permit access to the crosshead, slidebars and piston assembly. Alexander Allan had worked for George Forrester at the Vauxhall Foundry, and he developed his design from some early locomotives built there for the Liverpool and Manchester; Dublin and Kingstown, and London and Greenwich Railways. He in due course made it the 'hallmark' of locomotives produced at Crewe Works, the first of these being *Columbine* built in February, 1845. Prior to this some engines of his type had been built in France under licence from him. Numerous versions of the basic *Crewe Type* were destined to appear, and it was still being developed on certain railways 30 years later as we shall see in a later chapter.

The *Crewe Type* were characterised by very neat little boiler mountings, in particular the single Salter valves, and in general they followed Stephenson's conception of simple straightforward finish, whilst possessing a distinctive character all their own.

Thus by the year 1851, just over 20 years since the opening of the Liverpool and Manchester Railway, the steam locomotive had been transformed from an unknown quantity gamely trying to prove its worth, to an accepted, and honoured, new influence upon everyday life in Britain. In the aesthetic sense it was rapidly becoming a classic of engineering skill and artistry combined, although the superb heights of 20 years hence tend nowadays to cloud our appreciation of this fact.

The Great Exhibition of 1851 was Britain's showplace for her new industrial skills. Amidst the appalling clutter of machine-made furniture and domestic items—all vainly imitating hand craftsmanship (like over-decorated birthday cakes in their tasteless richness of applied frills)—two shining examples stood out, pointing the way to true industrial design attitudes. One of these examples was the very building housing the exhibition, the Crystal Palace, with its honest use of iron and glass; the other example was there (for those willing to comprehend it) in the locomotives displayed to the crowds. Unfortunately the strange mood of the times—with its mixture of industrial vigour, associated squalor and wealth, together with an almost poetic, unreal, seeking of the picturesque —clouded the vision of most onlookers. Machinery, science and taste were things to be treated seriously, but in isolation; locomotives could be admired as feats of engineering; but surely *not* as things of beauty?

By 1851, locomotives were being constructed to increasingly large dimensions, with a view to obtaining greater power and improved performance. This was partly due to the results of the comparative trials arranged in 1846 by the Gauge Commission between locomotives of the Broad Gauge and Standard Gauge. The larger GWR locomotives had demonstrated their superiority over their standard gauge brethren in no uncertain manner, and locomotive builders were striving to obtain better results for the now standardised 4ft 8½in gauge.

14. The splendid *Plews* of the York, Newcastle and Berwick Railway, built by Hawthorn's in 1848. A most distinctive design of the period. Engine and tender are well matched, and the sweeping curves of the cutaway driving wheel splasher are noteworthy.

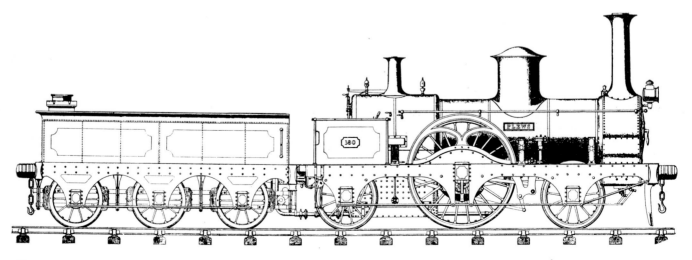

One of the locomotives exhibited at the Great Exhibition in Hyde Park was a GWR Broad Gauge 4–2–2, the *Lord of the Isles*, an example of the 8ft single *Iron Duke* class designed by Daniel Gooch. This type was destined to remain in service, through successive batches and renewals, until the end of the broad gauge in 1892; in itself a remarkable tribute to the sound principles of design Gooch had developed at Swindon. The *Iron Duke* class was developed from a locomotive built by Gooch in 1846, at a time when the 'Battle of the Gauges' was attracting considerable attention, and he intended it to demonstrate the superiority of the broad gauge. This 'one-off' locomotive was apparently scratch-built, without proper working drawings, and was the first locomotive entirely constructed at Swindon. With the appropriate name *Great Western*, it was a 2–2–2 with sandwich frames and a large Gothic firebox. Although it came up to expectations and performed well, it proved heavy at the leading end, and the front axle eventually broke, causing a derailment whilst the locomotive was hauling a train. As a result the front end framing was extended and an additional carrying axle was placed underneath; the wheelbase was rigid. The *Iron Duke* class adopted this 4–2–2 wheel arrangement, and had a domeless boiler, raised round-topped firebox with polished brass valve casing, and a huge chimney with a very handsome polished cap which set the whole design off to perfection. Strong influence of the original Stephenson *North Star* (and its *Patentee* origin) and the subsequent Gooch *Firefly* class, can be seen in these massive locomotives, with their restrained but satisfying aspect, with beautiful bright metalwork detailing. One feature of interest was the provision of a hooded seat in a raised position at the rear of the low sided tender, to accommodate and shelter the 'porter' who acted as guard to the train.

The important point to remember is that these broad gauge engines were truly massive, nearly twice the size of the standard gauge types. No wonder Brunel and Gooch were confident in the superiority of their locomotives—they were world beaters!

An interesting attempt to produce a standard gauge equivalent to

15, *above.* Frequently cited as the most beautiful design of the period was David Joy's *Jenny Lind,* designed for E. B. Wilson of Leeds. This type saw service on a number of British railways; the example illustrated was built for the Midland Railway in 1852. The classical treatment of dome and safety valve column was a hallmark of E. B. Wilson's products. **16,** *below,* shows these details, from an 0-6-0 goods locomotive built for the L.B.S.C.R.

17. A rare early photograph showing Crampton's *Kinnaird,* of the Dundee, Perth and Aberdeen Junction Railway, one of seven built by Tulk and Ley between 1846-1854. A Crampton engine possessed a totally different kind of aesthetic appeal, with the long wheel-base, and huge driving wheel set behind the firebox.

the *Iron Duke* class is seen in Archibald Sturrock's 7ft 6in 4–2–2 No. 215, built by R. & W. Hawthorn in 1853. Sturrock had gone to the Great Northern Railway from the Great Western Railway, and a good deal of Swindon influence can be seen in the general lines of 215, plus a few characteristic Hawthorn touches. She was before her time, and too heavy and large for the requirements of the day on the Great Northern, destined to remain the sole example of her class; but a most impressive machine to gaze upon.

From 1850 onwards the various experiments of the 'forties gave way to a more stable period of design. Many railways favoured the double-framed outside bearing, inside cylinder type; also the *Jenny Lind* variety, with inside bearings on the driving axle. Although some builders continued to feature elaborate ornamental flourishes—such as E. B. Wilson and Hawthorn's—the trend was towards a more restrained approach with the emphasis on clean lines and flowing curves, with details handled in an unobtrusive manner.

Two notable exceptions to the general trend of design were the McConnell *Bloomers* of the London and North Western Railway (Southern Division), and the outside cylinder locomotives of the *Crewe Type.* There were also outside cylinder locomotives of new designs on the London and South Western Railway during the period, but in general little progress was made with this type for some years.

The McConnell *Bloomers* broke away completely from the low centre of gravity theories of the 'forties, and in many ways they were advanced machines for their day. They had a bold, tall, outline with a high running plate, inside frames and bearings and inside cylinders. The nickname ' bloomer ' derived from the fact that they were considered to show rather a lot of leg (or rather wheel!) at a time when a certain Mrs. Amelia Bloomer was seeking reform in women's dress. There were extra large, large and small varieties of *Bloomers*—the locomotive, not the garment—and they must have presented a truly brave spectacle to mid-Victorian eyes, for not only did they have singularly elegant polished brass boiler mountings, they were painted a brilliant vermilion red. A notable advance in design was the tender for these engines, which was six-wheeled, with outside plate frames with slots cut out between the axleboxes, and springs placed below the platform or footplate level. Some featured india-rubber springs.

As already stated, double frames were a common feature of the period, producing an appearance which can aptly be described as the ' solid base ' type. For four-coupled and six-coupled locomotives, inside cylinders, double frames and outside cranks were the usual features; exceptions were those of McConnell on the LNWR. The Midland Railway Kirtley Goods locomotives of 1852 had outside plain plate frames instead of the sandwich variety introduced by Stephenson. The 2–4–0 wheel arrangement was coming into more general use, a particularly interesting example being the outside-cylinder variety introduced by Beattie for goods work on the London and South Western Railway in 1855.

Some scant consideration was now shown to the engine crew, with provision of a frontal weatherboard with two porthole windows. These must have been welcomed despite the meagre shelter they afforded, because trains were now travelling quite fast and the consequent slipstream must have fairly whistled past the footplate. Enginemen

18. Alexander Allan's *Crewe Type*. This example is 2-2-2 No. 7 of the Scottish Central Railway. Note the arrangement of front-end framing and cylinders. The single Salter safety valves were another characteristic feature. The primitive cab was a later addition, and is remarkable for the provision of an overhead roof.

19, *above.* Engines of Daniel Gooch's 'FIREFLY' class, Broad gauge 2-2-2's with huge polished brass 'Gothic' firebox casing, in the engine house at Swindon. Lithographed by J. C. Bourne.

20, *below.* 'IRON DUKE' class 4-2-2, *Hirondelle.* The hooded shelter on the rear of tender was for the 'porter'. From a scale model.

21. Archibald Sturrock's solitary No. 215 for the Great Northern Railway, built by R. & W. Hawthorn, 1853. Considerable Swindon influence is apparent in the overall design, with some characteristic Hawthorn touches added (particularly the driving wheel splasher).

at this time were a hardy lot who seemed to positively enjoy the spartan existence they led, but this weatherboard, or spectacle plate, seems to have been accepted quite readily by them, although they were to scorn the roomy cabs, complete with roof, of later years (*see ante*). The weatherboard was of minimal proportions, and the cab sides remained completely open above the waist level side sheets. Another change in detail design during the mid-fifties was the smokebox door, which had usually been of double folding type (see page 26), these began to give way to single doors of circular dished type (actually used on some Stephenson locomotives of the late 'forties, and probably invented by that firm); some railways continued to use doors of semi-circular Gooch type, which opened upwards about a horizontal hinge. The LNWR persisted with this type until the 1880's, an example is clearly seen in the illustration of a DX Goods (page 27). Other design changes included the use of metal boiler casings in place of wooden lagging strips, and spring instead of dumb buffers.

The locomotive of 1855 still owed much to Stephenson's *Patentee* of 20 years previously, but it had the benefits of refinement in manufacture, and considerably increased dimensions and capabilities. For express passenger work the single-driver wheel arrangement remained a favourite for the time being.

Between 1855–59 the principal changes were the introduction of *express* engines with four-coupled wheels (as opposed to previous goods designs), and increased use of bogies. The leading bogie had existed in a primitive form by 1849, on some 4–4–0 tank engines of the Great Western and South Devon Railways, to a design by Gooch which was perpetuated on the GWR for many years afterwards. Further attempts to use bogies were now made but the short wheelbase and frame, and lack of flexibility they had, hindered progress. In 1859 the London and South Western made a significant move by abandoning single wheelers in favour of four-coupled locomotives for express duties, and produced a 2–4–0 design built at Nine Elms with coupled wheels no less than 7ft in diameter.

Prior to this, 1854 must be noted as a significant year in the aesthetic development of the British steam locomotive, with the founding of the locomotive builders, Beyer Peacock and Company. From the outset this firm produced designs of remarkable beauty, and the standards set were destined to have far reaching influences on locomotive design at home and abroad. In terms of detail finish a Beyer product was a definitely superior item, and one of the most notable features was the superb chimney, which had a distinct taper, being narrower at the top than the bottom, with a lovely polished cap. At the time of their introduction most builders were still using parallel chimneys, but Stephenson's and Sharp's had a similar taper, but not somehow of quite the same distinctive quality.

By the late 'fifties there were already signs of a move away from the 'solid base' type of locomotive, although examples were to continue to appear for a good many years to come, particularly on the GWR which long favoured the iron and wood sandwich frame for the better ride it produced on their tracks. The reliable 0–6–0 goods engine, a truly British creation, attained about this period the final characteristics it was to continue to hold for almost a further century of steam locomotive design and construction. This remarkable 'maid of all work', as it has often been described, became the dependable standby of most of our railway companies, performing all manner of work ranging from local freight duties to emergency use as an express passenger engine. Countless hundreds were built to a basically simple rugged design, with inside cylinders and solid inside slab frames, with gradual increase in size and efficiency through the years. A striking portent of its usefulness was the mass production of no less than 857 standardised examples of Ramsbottom's DX goods 0–6–0 for the London and North Western

22. A typical 2-2-2 express engine of the 1850's, built by Robert Stephenson & Co., for the Midland Railway. Compared with the *Jenny Lind* (plate 15) the outline is more restrained, with very simple treatment for dome cover and safety valve casing.

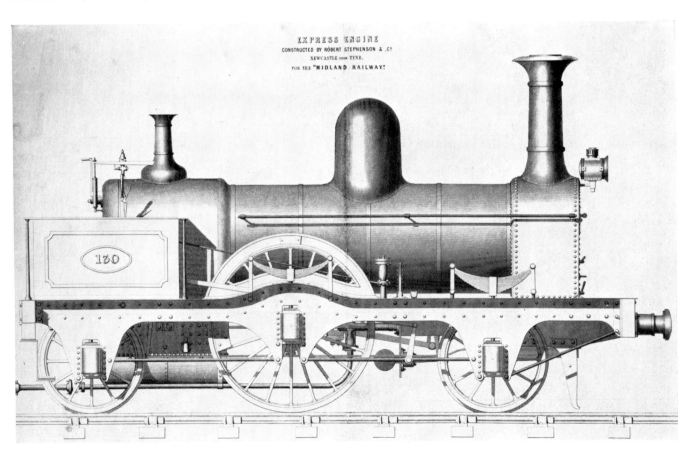

Railway between 1858–1872; with a further 86 produced for the Lancashire and Yorkshire Railway. This early case of mass production to a standardised design was an important contribution by Ramsbottom, who had succeeded Allan at Crewe. Not only were locomotives of the same class standard, but many parts were interchangeable between classes. Policy at Crewe was one of small engines, cheaply built but robust and simple to maintain and operate. Not for Crewe the elaborate brass domes and valve casings of McConnell at Wolverton; a plain severe outline was the order of the day, but nevertheless quite pleasing.

By way of contrast to the standard simplicity of Crewe, the London and South Western Railway had some remarkable gadgetry attached to its locomotives around this time, due to the apparent love of their designer, Joseph Beattie, for experiments with patent devices to improve his basically straightforward machines. Some ran with a sort of extra chimney, or even two extra, of slender proportions erected in front of the chimney proper, and there were all manner of pipes, wheels and handles festooned about the boiler and firebox. For all this apparent inventiveness the locomotives were basically very good looking machines.

Between 1860 and 1865 the existing locomotive types were enlarged and improved, with only a few innovations. In Scotland, Benjamin Connor produced some 8ft singles, with outside cylinders, for the Caledonian Railway (1859–1865) which had definite affinities with the Allan *Crewe Type* (of which numerous examples existed in Scotland), but with the cylinders placed horizontally, not inclined. Crewe's own contemporaries to these Scottish relatives were the *Problem* or *Lady of the Lake* class, of which 60 were constructed. These had more advanced features, with inside frames, inside bearings and outside cylinders. In common with other locomotives of similar wheel arrangement, the big single driving wheel was housed in a 'paddlebox' splasher, with a pattern of cutaway slots.

A further derivative of the *Crewe Type* appeared on the Great Eastern Railway in 1862 to a design by Robert Sinclair. Although these showed many Allan features they are noteworthy for two details incorporated. One was the plain stovepipe chimney, a hallmark of Sinclair, which was copied by Connor and Brittain on the Caledonian Railway. The other feature was the provision of quite a generous cab design, which after some initial distrust won the men's acceptance. Other railways to produce 'singles' at this time included the Midland, the Great Northern and the South Eastern. Further types of 2–4–0 appeared, but perhaps the most interesting types of the period were the passenger engines with leading bogies, most designed by Stephenson & Co., of which six for the Stockton and Darlington Railway are particularly noteworthy.

23. McConnell's celebrated 'BLOOMERS' of the L.N.W.R. (Southern Division), broke completely away from the low centre of gravity theories of the 1840's. These singularly handsome locomotives were painted vermilion red with highly polished brass fittings. Their high running plate and exposed wheels earned them their curious nickname. This example is 'SMALL BLOOMER' No. 103, built Wolverton 1857. (See plate 83, for a detail showing the men's uniforms.)

This page:

24. A characteristic Hawthorn product. Engine No. 69 of the Great North of England Railway, at Richmond (Yorks.) station. Note the shapely weatherboard, also the old style of double-folding smokebox doors.

Opposite page:

25, *top.* Locomotive *Fitzwilliam* of the South Yorkshire Railway, *circa* 1855. An inside-cylinder mixed-traffic 0-4-2.

26, *bottom.* London & North Western Railway Ramsbottom DX GOODS No. 1080, in original condition. Photographed at the old Manchester (Victoria) station in 1868, by G. T. Rhodes. Note the Ramsbottom ornamental chimney cap, and the Gooch-type smokebox door with hinge uppermost.

The initial two, with bogie wheels of 3ft 6in diameter and 6ft coupled wheels, were built in anticipation of the opening of the line from Barnard Castle to Tebay, over the exposed Pennine Hills, and were named *Brougham* and *Lowther*, after the residences of Lord Brougham and Lord Lonsdale. They had outside cylinders and inside frames, with a long bogie frame, and in many ways they were advanced locomotives for their time, foreshadowing the designs of late Victorian years. Most remarkable of all was the provision of a large spacious cab, complete with side windows (discussed later), but it seems these were not favourably received by the stalwart drivers, as the following four engines of the class reverted to open footplates with merely the front weatherboards for protection.

Another 4–4–0 type was introduced in 1864–65, by Edward Fletcher for the North Eastern Railway, to work on the severely curved Whitby–Malton route. These 'Whitby bogies' seem to have been a successful design for the job, and they lasted some 25 years on it, but aesthetically they were very weak, with the small-wheeled, short framed bogie cramped beneath the front end. Only the flowing lines of the big dome casing, with its Salter valves, catches our eye, and this was a fairly typical style of the times, although Fletcher's version seemed even more curvacious than most. But these 4–4–0 ventures were exceptions and another 10 years was to pass before the bogie passenger engine really came into its own. However, by the end of 1866 most of the leading railways had discontinued new construction of 'singles'—except the GNR and GWR—although of course many hundreds of examples were in everyday use. As we shall see in a later chapter there was to be a single revival, when steam sanding was introduced. The four coupled express engine was gaining favour, but not as yet with a leading bogie.

As mentioned above, the Great Northern Railway was an exception to the trend, due to the arrival on the scene of Patrick Stirling, who took charge of the Locomotive Department in 1866. Previously he had been with the Glasgow and South Western Railway, at Kilmarnock, and there he had developed his own 'single' designs, and he arrived at his new post determined to adhere to the 'single'. Back in 1857 he had produced a 2–2–2 at Kilmarnock with outside cylinders, a domed boiler and inside frames. This little engine bore a remarkable resemblance to the later *Lady of the Lake* design of Ramsbottom's at Crewe. A later

series of 2–2–2 engines built for the GSWR, between 1860–1868 had outside cylinders, domeless boilers and some of the class had the first examples of the round-topped cab that Stirling made a feature of his designs. In these locomotives we see the progenitors of the famous 8ft outside cylinder 4–2–2 of 1870 (see Chapter Five). For his first designs on the Great Northern Railway, Stirling reverted to inside cylinders with domeless boilers and round topped cabs producing first 2–4–0's and then 'singles'. The plain outline, relieved only by shapely safety valve casing, of the domeless boiler and flush firebox; the simple but effective cab design and the general lack of fuss in detailing of these locomotives of the late 'sixties, serve admirably to show how locomotive design was becoming more and more a true piece of industrial art—a marriage of function and appearance. Patrick Stirling was one of several locomotive engineers who were becoming increasingly aware that a locomotive could be handsome in itself, and did not require elaborate ornamentation to render it appealing to the eye.

Mention has been made above of several attempts to offer improved cabs to enginemen, in particular the spacious examples on the first two Stockton and Darlington Railway 4–4–0's built by Stephenson's. It seems strange that the men themselves should oppose such amenities, but this was in fact the case. The driver of 1860 was a fiercely proud individual, with dignified bearing, a deeply bronzed weatherbeaten face and in all probability a large beard. This appendage served him well on cold winter nights, and many are the tales of drivers arriving at their destination with large particles of ice in their beards, practically frozen stiff on the footplate! Such men would not take kindly at first to any suggestions of softening-up their conditions. But other factors played their part in the quite heated debate on the pros and cons of cabs. One of these was a suspicion voiced by some locomotive superintendents that if the drivers were too comfortable some would be prone to fall asleep on duty! Another factor was vandalism—which unfortunately

27. Some of Beattie's patent gadgetry on his 2-4-0 *Atalanta,* of the 'UNDINE' class. 1859/60.

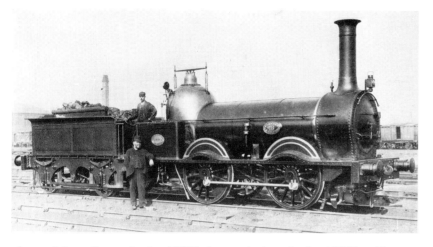

28. Somewhat remarkable was the perpetuation of Edward Bury's small bar-framed designs until 1861, on the Furness Railway. No. 16 was built by W. Fairbairn & Sons.

plagued the railways in the 1860's just as it does in the 1960's. Ahrons, in his book ' The British Steam Locomotive from 1825 to 1925 ', states the following :

' On the Midland Railway in 1863 some boys threw bricks down from an over-bridge at Loughborough, severely injuring the driver, after which Kirtley gave better protection by bending the top of the weatherboard completely over the footplate, supporting it at the back by means of two columns. This form of weatherboard rattled when the engine was running, and the 20 engines or so fitted with it were known as the " drummers ". The drivers objected strongly to it, and asked for its removal. A compromise was reached whereby the weather-board was bent over only part of the footplate and was not supported by pillars. This arrangement was standard until 1872 on the Midland.'

The important point is that gradual acceptance of better shelter on the part of the enginemen was being won, and the designs of Patrick Stirling and Benjamin Connor pointed the way to future development, with a sensible protection overhead as well as to the front and sides, although the time had not yet come when men would accept the ' modern ' fully enclosed footplate that Stephenson's had used on the Stockton and Darlington engines of 1860 !

By the end of the period reviewed in this chapter, the British steam locomotive had assumed definite characteristics, which may be described as a subtle combination of neatness, simplicity, harmonious lines and fitness for purpose. It was on the whole already an attractive machine, but some even more encouraging portents for the future could be seen in the shape of some early 2–4–0 locomotives by Samuel Johnson on the Great Eastern Railway, in the Stirlings of the Great Northern and in some rebuildings of early Allan engines by a certain Mr. William Stroudley on the far-off Highland Railway. Nor should we overlook the important contribution to locomotive aesthetics that Beyer Peacock and Company were already making.

Finally a word on locomotive liveries during the formative years. To begin with these were a matter for the fancy of the individual loco-motive engineers. At the time of the Rainhill Trials Stephenson's *Rocket* was painted bright yellow with a white chimney, a colour scheme which one suspects was most carefully chosen to make his little engine more appealing to eyes as yet unaccustomed to steam locomotives. The chief competitor to *Rocket* in the popularity stakes, was the dainty little *Novelty* which had an elegance all its own, and this was painted with blue frames and wheels, set-off by a polished copper boiler casing. The other two contestants—the aptly named *Perseverance* and Hackworth's elephantine *Sans Pareil*—both displayed little concern for appearance.

Locomotive builders soon adopted their own individual liveries, helping to distinguish their products which were seen thus on various railways. But by the late 'forties railways had become sufficiently numerous and closely grouped to make some form of distinctive *company* livery desirable. Locomotives began to appear in uniform colours, but

29, *above.* A *Crewe Type* derivative. Benjamin Connor's 8ft. single for the Caledonian Railway, the first of which was constructed at St. Rollox in 1859. No. 83A is shown here in later days, with alterations including a Drummond chimney. The driving wheel splasher had no less than twenty-two slots cut into it.

30, *below.* J. Ramsbottom's 'PROBLEM' class No. 531, *Lady of the Lake.* Photographed outside Crewe works where she was built in May 1862.

not as yet bearing much else to show who they belonged to, except the running number and perhaps some initials.

Conventions soon arose, with certain colours definitely preferred for certain parts of the locomotive. Black was invariably used for smoke-box and chimney casing, frames were most often in a deep brown, red or similar shade. Boilers, sidesheets and tender sides were in brighter shades with green a great favourite. But deep blues, purple-browns and indian reds were also popular. A few railways chose really striking colours, most notably the vermilion red of the London and North Western Railway, Southern Division. Some special engines appeared in 'fancy' livery, such as the 'Royal' Crampton of the North British Railway, finished in Tartan overall!

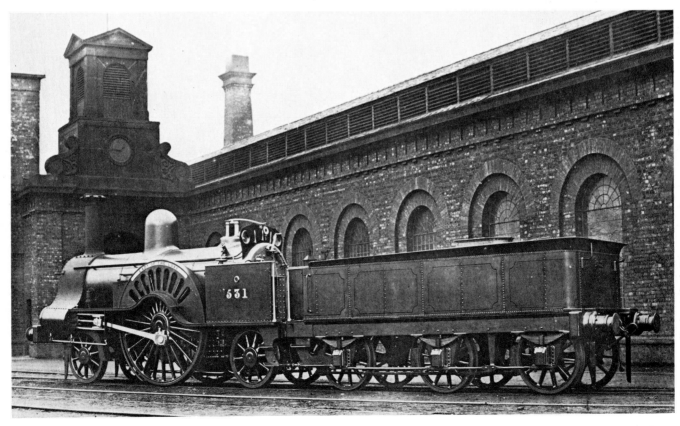

The basic colours were invariably relieved by ' lining-out ', often in black and white, gilt, orange or red, or a combination of three or more of these. Yellow and pale green were also favourites for lining purposes. The practice of emphasising panelling by the painting was entirely logical, it drew the eye away from rows of rivet heads, metal bands and other constructional details. The outer surrounds of the panels would be in a dark colour separated by lining from the lighter colour within. A favourite style of ' lining-out ' in mid-Victorian times had the corners cut off by reversed quarter circles. Buffer beams were usually vermilion, although this was sometimes confined to a central panel surrounded by the darker colour used for the frames.

Great care was taken with the finished appearance of locomotives, all metal working surfaces were finished bright and kept polished and oiled, and copper and brass fittings were highly polished. Varnishing was an elaborate process, very necessary to protect the pigments beneath. All these aspects are dealt with in greater detail in Chapter Eight.

31, *top.* J. I. Cudworth's smart 2-4-0 standard design for the South Eastern Railway, of which over 100 were built between 1859-1875 with only minor modifications.

32, *lower left.* Caledonian Railway 2-4-0 No. 41, another *Crewe Type* derivative. Note the "stovepipe" chimney and shapely cab.

33, *lower right.* A pioneer bogie 4-4-0. Edward Fletcher's 'WHITBY BOGIE' of 1864/65, for the North Eastern Railway's severely curved line between Whitby and Malton. A clumsy design with lack of balance to the overall proportions.

2 | Travelling on the Railway

The coming of railways spelt slow but certain death to the mail and stagecoaches which had plied the roads of Britain. At the same time it opened-up new opportunities for travel to all classes of society, including the poorest who had previously either travelled just as far as their own two feet could take them; or else perhaps had travelled on one of the slow, lumbering stage waggons. For the wealthy, already accustomed to more frequent travelling, and often possessing their own chaise or coach, the railway was an acceptable equivalent if one travelled first class. Despite this, for some time many preferred the privacy of their own horse-drawn vehicle, and for rail journeys they remained in it whilst it was hauled along the line mounted upon a flat carriage truck.

For those who had previously endured long road journeys seated 'outside', the railway alternative of an open carriage with seats, was quite feasible. For the really poor, an open carriage *without* seats would bear comparison to the discomforts of a stage waggon—and the journey was far quicker!

Such then were the conditions of rail travel considered suitable by the directors of the earliest passenger railways, and one must acknowledge the period of social upheaval that Britain was going through at that time, with its very positive strata of society, to appreciate the fact that to begin with at least no-one saw anything very strange or wrong in the vastly different travelling conditions offered on the railway, to different classes.

As mentioned in Chapter One, the promoters of the Liverpool and Manchester Railway had the conveyance of goods between those two cities as the uppermost thought in their minds. Much to their surprise when the line opened, the volume of passenger traffic soon exceeded the volume and value of goods consignments, and they were pressed to order more passenger rolling stock to meet the demand.

The earliest carriages built for the line had included some weird and wonderful experiments, (for who could say *exactly* what a railway carriage should be?), but the demand for additional stock enabled the lessons to be quickly learned, and by 1834 a clearer solution to the requirements was emerging.

A contemporary account of two of the original 1830 designs, from 'An Accurate Description, etc.', by J. S. Walker, is worth quoting:

> 'The most costly and elegant contain three apartments, and resemble the body of a coach (in the middle) and two chaises, one at each end—the whole joined together. Another resembles an oblong square of church pews, panelled at each end, and the rail which supports the back so contrived that it may be turned over, so that the passengers may face either way, and the machine does not require to be turned.'

The first passenger carriages for the Liverpool and Manchester line were on waggon style underframes with four wheels and cantilever springs as on road coaches. It was not at first considered necessary to provide any form of lighting or heating, or to make any sanitary provision. A slight acknowledgement to the unpredictable nature of English

34. The first passenger carriage, built 1825 for for the opening of the Stockton and Darlington Railway. Purely functional; rather like a garden shed upon wheels.

weather was made in the open carriages by the provision of numerous holes in the floor to allow rain-water to drain away—and of course allow draughts up the legs of travellers therein! The riding qualities of these short wheelbase, loose coupled carriages, with their padded leather buffers to take the shocks of starting and stopping, can be only too readily imagined.

The resemblance of the covered first class carriage (with three six-seater compartments containing well padded seat cushions, arm rests and padded back, and with droplights in the doors, with quarter-lights each side) to an enlarged road coach, has often been remarked upon. This was quite logical, and certainly must have helped to promote the idea of travel on the railway in the minds of the wealthier classes, by presenting a familiar aspect to a new mode of travel. Moreover it must be remembered that coach building was an art in itself, requiring skilled craftsmen, and one can appreciate the readiness of railway engineers such as the Stephensons to hand this department over to those best equipped, whilst they tackled the problems of locomotive development and other aspects of railway engineering. The employment of the coach-builder Nathaniel Worsdell to construct a tender for Stephenson's *Rocket*, has already been remarked upon—what more fitting choice could be made when the problem of providing suitable passenger carriages arose? Besides which, the coachbuilders must have welcomed the new source of work the railway offered, for the road coaches were threatened by railway competition.

Externally the coachbuilder's traditions were carried most completely on to the first class railway carriages, with the characteristic panelling and curved quarterlights retained to each compartment. The nearly flat roof had railings enclosing a luggage space and there was often a seat on the roof for the guard to travel on, as in the days of road coaches. The second and third class railway carriages were derived more from the road waggon, rather than coachbuilding, practice. When, after some years, second class passengers were provided with coach-style carriages these lacked the quarterlights, but many had open sides

35, *above.* A later (1846) Stockton and Darlington carriage, clearly showing road coach influence. The interior, **36,** *below,* of the first class compartment is fairly typical of the period. Note the hole in the ceiling for a pot-oil lamp, and the silk cords to hang top-hats by the brim. These compartments were the progenitors of the typical British compartment carriage design.

37, *right.* Birmingham and Derby Junction Railway carriage. The bodywork has a more rectangular character than was typical, but otherwise this drawing illustrates clearly the general arrangement.

38, *below.* The interior of a first class compartment of the 1840's-1850's. Note the headrests between seats, together with padded armrests. Also the buttoned upholstery. An excellent contemporary painting, by Abraham Solomons, entitled 'The Return'; exhibited at the 1854 Royal Academy.

above the waists with a canopy above and curtains that could be drawn across for protection.

In the compartment layout of the first class carriage of the mid 1830's, which was only some 6ft high inside and not much more than 5ft wide, we nevertheless have the progenitor of the typical British non-corridor compartment carriage, of which countless thousands have been produced over a period of 120 years.

Mention has been made already of the provision of a box seat on the roof for a guard. One of the guard's duties was to act as a brakesman and he was one of several stationed along the length of the train, which at first possessed no continuous brakes. From their elevated position they could observe signals from the lineside or the locomotive, meanwhile receiving more than their fair share of cinders and smuts in common with the poor unfortunates in the open carriages.

Improvements in the buffers and couplings between carriages, were soon made, and the stock of 1834 (as exemplified by the beautiful replica of the first class carriage *Experience* now in the Museum of British Transport at Clapham), was equipped with spring buffering and drawgear with screw couplings. This must have considerably lessened the amount of jolting and jarring. There is also about this design a certain new elegance, one point removed from road coach practice, which has a familiar aspect to our eyes. In fact, with its repetitive, evenly spaced rectangular window arrangement, it begins to look like a railway carriage !

When the London and Birmingham Railway opened to passenger business during 1837–38, the company chose to remain faithful to the conventions of the Liverpool and Manchester for passenger carriage design. At the time of the opening of the first section, from Euston to Boxmoor, on July 20th, 1837, the company provided the following amenities (to quote their advertisement) :

'First class coaches carry six passengers inside, and each seat is numbered.
Second class coaches carry eight passengers inside, and are covered, but without lining, cushions or divisions, and the seats are not numbered.
Third class coaches carry four passengers on each seat, and are without covering.'

(It should be pointed out that the numbers of passengers of first and second class referred to in that extract, as 'inside', are those *per compartment*.)

C. Hamilton Ellis, in his splendid book ' Railway Carriages in the British Isles from 1830 to 1914 ', reminds us that the punnish nickname of *Stanhopes* was bestowed upon the ' stand-up ' third class opens. A long train of *Stanhopes* can be seen on the left hand side of the illustration of Euston Station (page 43).

An early, and very amusing description of railway travel is entitled ' The Railway Monitor ' and says :

' *To Travellers.*

The existing railway arrangements render it imperative that you should provide yourself with a large stock of philosophy, to enable you to put up with certain inconveniences, which you will be sure, to a greater or less extent, to encounter on most lines, and whereof a classification is hereby appended for your benefit.

First Class

The chief inconvenience peculiar to this class is that your fare will be about twice as much as you ought in fairness to pay. You run, perhaps, rather less risk in this class than in the others, of having your neck broken ; but you must not be unprepared for such a contingency.

Second Class

In travelling by the second class, you will do well to wear a respirator, unless you wish to be choked with dust and ashes from the engine close in front of you. Also, if you are going far, you are recommended to put on a diving-dress . . . because, if it should rain much during your journey, the sides of the carriage being open you will have to ride in a pool of water. Your dignity must not be hurt, should you have for next neighbour a ragamuffin in handcuffs, with a policeman next him. The hardness of your seat is a mere trifle ; that is the least of the annoyances to which you are judiciously subjected, with the view of driving you into the first-class train.

Third Class

Make up your mind for unmitigated hail, rain, sleet, snow, thunder and lightning. Look out for a double allowance of smoke, dust, dirt, and everything that is disagreeable. Be content to run a twofold risk of loss of life and limbs. Do

39. All the delights of a sea-side bound excursion train, South Eastern Railway 1844. Fortunately the sun is shining ! This charming drawing appeared on the cover of a popular piece of music of the day.

40. An iron bodied third class carriage of the mid 1840's, for the Vale of Neath Railway, which later went to the G.W.R. The nearly flat iron roof afforded some degree of protection against the elements. A true horror of a carriage, it nevertheless survived long enough to be converted to a milk van in 1870, lasting as such until 1887.

not expect the luxury of a seat. As an individual and a traveller, you are one of the lower classes; a poor, beggarly, contemptible person, and your comfort and convenience are not to be attended to.'

Carriages on the 7ft gauge Great Western Railway were, from the start, of definitely superior vein to their smaller contemporaries—at least, for the first class passengers in which it was predominantly interested. For second class it provided some closed and some open carriages, whilst for a class described as 'persons in lower stations of life' travel was in uncovered trucks in the goods trains. Brunel had recommended the use of six-wheeled carriages and these were subsequently ordered for the first class. Although, in common with the earlier railways' first class stock, the first class compartments were only 6ft high, they were no less than 9ft 6in wide, and there were four compartments each seating eight passengers. Upholstery was in Morocco leather, and a noteworthy feature was the provision of ventilation louvres above the windows. Some compartments had a central longitudinal partition with a glazed door, which gave a greater degree of privacy to the two sets of four seats. A special type of carriage, introduced by the Great Western in its early days was the 'Posting Carriage', notable for the saloon layout (a sort of room on rails) and clerestory type of roof. Hamilton Ellis states that they were intended as a sort of extra first class, with an internal arrangement of two U-shaped leather sofas, surrounding card tables, and a central porch with door, each side. Public response to this layout was poor, probably due in part to the fact that they were badly ventilated and rough riding (they were four-wheelers whereas the ordinary firsts were six-wheeled), and they were soon demoted to less frequent use as party or family saloons. Perhaps the most interesting feature of these 'Posting Carriages' was the clerestory roof, which gave increased headroom and better natural lighting. This seems to have been the first railway essay in this architectural form, which was to be used to great effect in the later years of the nineteenth century; but for the time being the idea did not catch on.

In August, 1844, Gladstone's Railway Regulation Act received the Royal Assent. This obliged the railway companies to provide weatherproof travelling accommodation for third class passengers, once a day. Many companies literally obeyed the word of the law and provided one such train a day, but at night or else in the early hours of the morning—thereby doing their best to discourage third class travel. These unearthly timed trains became known as the 'Parliamentary trains' and their slow and weary progress through the countryside was matched only by the cramped, unlit, and poorly ventilated carriages used. This well intentioned Act of Parliament did not abolish the old open

41. Interior of the special smoking saloon introduced in 1846 by the Eastern Counties Railway.

Stanhopes; on the contrary, they were utilised for passengers foolish enough to choose third class travel on trains other than the one 'Parliamentary' a day! They were also used for excursion traffic; presumably a trip to the seaside could be a reasonably gay affair in one of these open carriages—weather permitting.

However, the Act did force the companies to improve their second class accommodation, and low partitions divided these into semi-compartments, with covered bodies, but poor ventilation and illumination remained their lot.

To begin with, first class passengers desirous of lighting facilities brought these with them, in the form of an individual candle in a holder which could be hooked to a suitable spot on the compartment wall close to their heads. But by the early 1840's lamps burning rape oil were used in some carriages. Placed in position through a hole in the roof, the lamps could be removed as necessary for refilling. The waterproofing of these potholes was not very effective, and sorry was the plight of passengers should the lamp not have been replaced properly on a wet and stormy night! Some companies decided that one lamp might well be shared by two compartments if it were placed in a position cut-out of the wall between the two. The housings for these rape oil lamps were a prominent feature on the roofs of carriages so equipped. On some of the enclosed third class carriages introduced as a result of Gladstone's Act, one lamp sufficed to illuminate the whole carriage, which was of open layout crammed with bench seats. Another innovation was provision of heating in cold weather, by means of hot water footwarmers.

Smoking by passengers was generally discouraged by the early railway companies on their trains and stations, but by 1846 attitudes were evidently changing, because the Eastern Counties Railway introduced a special smoking saloon in that year, and later on special

42. A former fourth class carriage of the Brighton Railway, *circa* 1860. Originally it would have had open sides above the waist. As depicted here it was probably used on 'Parliamentary' trains, as third class. A solitary oil lamp illuminated the interior.

compartments were set aside for smokers, by the various companies.

By the time of the 1851 Great Exhibition, development of railway passenger carriages lagged far behind the impressive progress in locomotive design, railway engineering and architecture. The reasons for this are not easily defined with certainty, but it seems that a good deal of the initial romance of travelling by train had been lost, and complaints of travelling conditions were voiced with increasing vigour. Sad to relate, there was not much improvement in carriage design over the next 10 years or so, and just to prove otherwise to all who imagined the railways had achieved the nadir with their third class, there were actually fourth class carriages in use on certain lines for excursions and cheap trips!

The construction of carriage bodies advanced slowly, with some increase in length (adding extra compartments) but this was limited by the rigid wheelbase used. The lighting was still rape oil, which offered dismal illumination at the best. Some improvement in the welfare of second class passengers was achieved with such luxuries as stiff cushions to sit upon and quarterlight windows flanking the door. The first class remained stodgily comfortable, with panels and mouldings picked out rather crudely in gold; probably a mirror; ponderous buttoned-in upholstery; curtains, and a carpet. The inside of the door would usually be padded with a thick buttoned leather squab. The exterior was beginning to lose its road coach ancestry and panelling was more rectangular with possibly a curved treatment remaining at each end of the carriage side. Slotted 'venetian' ventilators were inserted above the windows.

Some increase in the width and height of carriages began to be noticeable in the 1860's, but there can have been little incentive to make any great improvements in this respect whilst lighting and heating remained so poor. Nevertheless six-wheeled carriages with larger bodies began to replace the four wheelers (although as we have seen, the GWR used six wheelers from the outset). Although a Mr. Joseph Wright had patented bogie carriage designs as early as 1844, British companies did not take up the idea for many years hence.

Sanitary facilities were unknown to ordinary passengers of any class, and at this time sleeping on a train was by means of an improvised arrangement of seat cushions across the compartment, with bed linen hired from the guard. Not many people availed themselves of this amenity, however, and for the majority of stalwarts who had perforce to journey overnight, rugs about the person were advisable.

A development of the late 'sixties was family saloon carriages (which met with greater success than the GWR 'Posting Carriage'

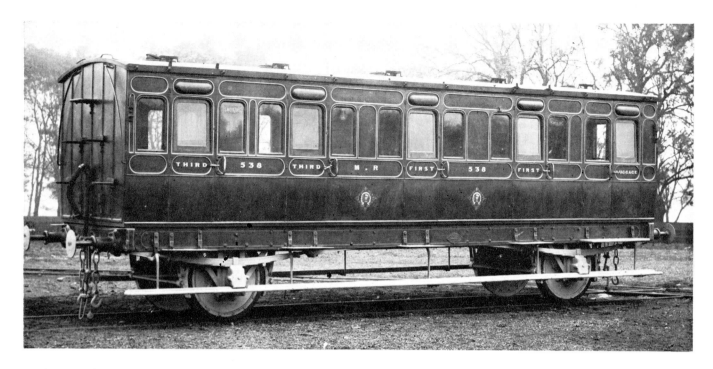

design mentioned earlier). Victorian families tended to be large, and the saloon layout catered well for these when travelling complete with servants. There was also the very desirable provision of toilet facilities—no doubt a large family blessed this! But for the present such sanitary provisions were the exception rather than the rule.

Enclosed carriages in early years followed road coach practice for their external liveries, as well as construction. The upper panels were usually black; the lower, yellow, green or red. Names were carried as in road coach days, and the general intention seems to have been to bestow as much familiarity as possible upon their outward aspect, in order to reassure passengers embarking upon their first rail journeys. Open carriages of third and second class would be a different colour (blue seems to have been a favourite) and the complete train would present quite a colourful assembly.

As time went on, a more uniform livery was selected by the individual companies, and the practice of naming carriages was dropped. Instead they were identified by numbers, and usually carried a mono-gram of the initials of the company, or possibly a coat of arms. Panelling was emphasised by 'lining-out' and painting the relief mouldings. It seems that quite early on it was realised that a more logical way of painting railway carriages (as opposed to road coaches) was to use a dark colour for panels below the waist and perhaps a light one for those above—or else a single dark colour overall. Traditional coach-building finishes were still followed, with great care taken over 'lining-out', which was often in gold leaf edged each side by a fine vermilion stripe. Varnishing completed the whole ensemble and this was applied by skilled hands to achieve an almost mirrorlike surface.

By 1870 rail travel was the fastest available means of transport in man's history; it was virtually without competitors—but it was by no means a pleasurable experience.

43. By the late 'sixties carriages were longer, but still low roofed. This Midland Railway example (photographed in 1874) was probably originally built as a composite first and second class, and later altered to first and "improved" third. Note the end luggage compartment.

3 | Railway Architecture

44. The triumphal Liverpool and Manchester Railway Moorish Arch, at Edge Hill, seen here in Shaw's contemporary etching of the opening ceremony, September 15th, 1830. Although greatly admired at the time, it was soon demolished. Note the elaborate carriages used to convey the guests (including the Duke of Wellington), on the left.

The development of railway architecture probably tells us more about the character of the men who pioneered Britain's railways than any other aspect. Indeed, the whole architecture of the Industrial Revolution is most revealing of the raw, vital, spirit of the times. In 1830 (as we have seen in Chapter One) the steam locomotive remained very much an unknown quantity which was to undergo a long period of mechanical development, from which a gradual sense of style emerged. Carriage design, we have also seen, was largely borrowed from the road coach-builder and placed upon rails, following which there was very little real advance in amenity for over a quarter of a century. But when we come to architecture we are dealing with one of the most ancient and highly developed arts of civilised man, and the way in which it was adapted to the requirements of the new railways was one of the most interesting aspects of Victorian life. It is in fact almost impossible to overstate the importance of this period, both for the many examples of exceptional quality it produced, and for the sense of stability, dignity and purpose architecture bestowed upon the new method of travel by rail.

Today we are still surrounded by the buildings of Victorian England, a legacy in bricks and mortar; in crowded industrial streets, factories, civic buildings and our canal and railway networks. To our eyes it seems often dowdy, grime encrusted and outdated, particularly when in close juxtaposition to new concrete-and-glass structures. To appreciate the true merits, and faults, it possesses, we must try to think back to the days when these buildings were bright and new—before the soot-laden atmosphere of nineteenth century England changed their face. Perhaps one day this country will learn to appreciate its architectural heritage and will institute a 'cleaning-up' operation comparable to that achieved by De Gaulle for Paris—then we would have our eyes opened!

Victorian railway architecture is exciting because it is full of contrasts; contrasts of style and treatment, of masterly handling of classic forms and of daring innovations in new media.

From the start there seems to have been a sense of adventure and of social occasion in railway architecture, and every opportunity was seized to build on an impressive scale when suitable occasions arose. Thus we have a number of large station buildings handled in the classical manner, with great dignity; for example Birmingham (Curzon Street), Brighton and Huddersfield. To these can be added such forthright statements of grandeur as the Moorish Arch of the Liverpool and Manchester Railway at Edge Hill, and the magnificent Doric portico at Euston—both symbols of a revolution, no less; built not for functional reasons but rather as gestures, just as Napoleon built his triumphal arches in France.

But behind these bold façades, handled with such superb confidence, there were totally new problems to be solved, and these were approached with admirable courage. Early solutions were tentative, but soon a positive conception was evolved. In this, I think particularly of

the problem of railway station design. This fell into two distinct halves; the 'office block' (containing ticket office, waiting rooms etc.) and the 'train shed' which accommodated the railway lines and allowed the passengers to board and alight.

The office block could be easily handled, being only one step removed from the conventions of civic and domestic architecture. But the train shed—as it became known—was a new problem, with its layout of railway lines and the need to control the people within. This division of office block and train shed, separated by a 'barrier' was to become a feature of our stations.

45, *above.* A sense of the great social importance of the new railways was imparted by the architecture of early large stations, most often by a classical treatment, with porticoes, colonnades, etc. Illustrated is Curzon Street, Birmingham, by Philip Hardwicke, 1838. On a much grander scale was the London terminus at Euston, **46,** *below,* which possessed great dignity, with the Doric arch flanked by lodges.

An awareness of social responsibility also seems to have ranked high in the minds of railway architects from the earliest days. Everything possible was done to make the new buildings, bridges, tunnels and viaducts ' belong ' to their surroundings, and to prevent the new railways offending the eye. Sometimes this resulted in the exterior of a relatively small and unimportant station or bridge being disproportionately grand, but research usually unearths a very good reason in such cases. We must remember that in many instances considerable opposition and resentment was experienced from powerful landlords when new railways were proposed and no doubt some tactful architectural solutions helped to win the day for the railways. Thus, stations and ancillary buildings were often designed to fit into, and enhance, the landscape; in fact many did this extremely well by adoption of existing vernacular styles.

Tunnel mouths, bridges and viaducts were given grand architectural treatment and many examples were singularly beautiful in proportion and details. Unfortunately the true beauty of the majority of these tunnel mouths is today hidden beneath the accumulated soot of a century and a quarter of steam locomotion, and our express trains speed into them so fast that we scarcely catch a glimpse. But picture to yourself the adventure of entering one of these long tunnels in the early days of steam, at a calm 30–35mph, and *no lights* in the carriages. How reassuring it must have been to have gazed upon the impressive portals of the tunnel entrance—a solid testimony of faith in these terrific engineering works.

Right from the start railway building was a fascinating blend of traditional styles and exciting new experiments. One reason was the need, already observed, to solve new problems unique to the layout of a railway. But another reason was the improvement in the manufacture of iron. We have seen how the steam locomotive progressed parallel to improved manufacturing methods, and better use of raw materials. The railway builders were quick to make use of this improved iron for structural solutions to such problems as the need to provide overhead verandahs, or roofs to the train sheds, at stations. There were large spaces to be covered over, and these had to be as free as possible from supports which could hinder the layout of lines below. Iron and glass were to become the basis of some magnificent solutions to this problem.

Wood had been considered a suitable material for the construction

47, *above.* Huddersfield, by James and Charles Pritchett, 1847, with a true portico attached to the front of the building, combining function with a sense of great dignity. Seen here in present day condition; badly in need of cleaning.

48, *below.* David Mocatta's Brighton station, 1841. An early example of the Italian manner which was to be widely used for the following decade.

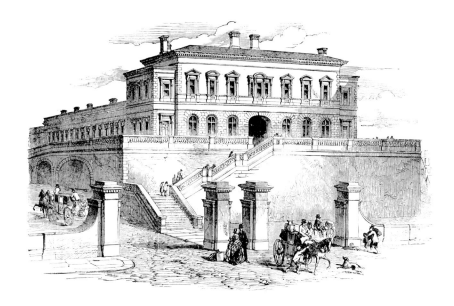

49. The new station at Tithebarn Street, Liverpool, opened in 1850. From a contemporary wood engraving.

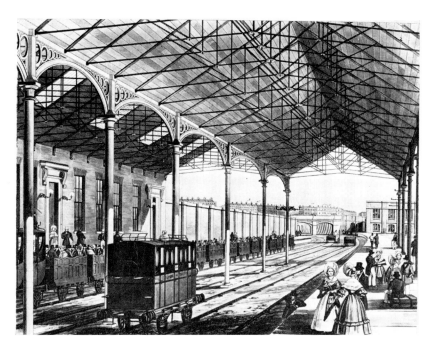

50. Compared to the magnificent approach, the actual trainshed at Euston was a simple unpretentious design; an early example of iron and glass station roof construction. Note the long train of 'STANHOPES', on the left of the picture. Etching by Bury.

51. The Shareholder's Meeting room at Euston station, completed in 1849 to the designs of P. C. Hardwick. Although less well known than the famous Great Hall at Euston, this room was perhaps even grander in manner.

52. Brunel's superb timber roof at Bristol Temple Meads; from a lithograph by J. C. Bourne.

of some of the earliest train sheds, and the examples at Bath and Bristol by Brunel represent the finest handling of the material. The roof at Bristol (Temple Meads) survives to this day; a great aisled nave with a hammerbeam timber roof resting upon Tudor style arches. But trains no longer stand beneath it—the area under this masterpiece has become a car park!

For the smaller stations the verandah style roof was quickly adopted, sometimes supported on columns on the platform (at first on the outer edge, later set back), and sometimes cantilevered out from the side of the station buildings. Iron was soon used extensively for the supports, and some very decorative treatments were produced which blended the verandah and station building together very well (see Chapter Seven).

By the mid 'forties railways were sufficiently large and widespread to create a need for much larger stations in major cities. From this need, and the greatly improved techniques of iron manufacture, arose the great series of iron roofs; beginning with Dobson's pioneer classic of Newcastle Central (1845) and quickly followed by Paddington (1854); Birmingham, New Street (1854); and Cannon Street (1866). In these great roofs we see a combination of architecture and engineering on a scale which marks it down as one of the greatest achievements of Victorian design. Paxton's Crystal Palace may have had the romance of the Great Exhibition to enhance its popularity, but Dobson's earlier Newcastle Central Station (which was probably a source of inspiration to Paxton) remains with us today, as impressive to the eye as it was the day it was completed, and still serving a useful purpose.

Paddington, produced by Mathew Digby Wyatt and Brunel, is another superb example which possesses a great sense of spaciousness and unity. To appreciate these great roofs at their finest, we would have

53, *left.* An early wayside station; Parkside on the Liverpool and Manchester Railway. Etching by Bury.

54, *centre.* Pangbourne, Great Western Railway. By the time the Broad gauge main line was constructed, a much clearer concept of country station design had evolved. The elegant shelter roofs are remarkably modern in appearance. Lithograph by J. C. Bourne.

55, *bottom.* Redhill, photographed in 1865. The roof is supported by slender cast-iron columns, placed outside the tracks. Note the early carriage, on the left, which is standing upon a cross-tracks traverser.

This page:

56, *right*. Brocklesby station, 1849, showing the arrival of Prince Albert for the laying of the foundation stone of Great Grimsby Docks. A charming exercise in Gable design, typical of many built in the Eastern counties about this time.

57, *below*. A perfect Gothic style station. Battle (Sussex), by William Tress, 1852.

Opposite page:

58, *top*. Interior of Paddington, by Brunel and Digby Wyatt, 1854. Superb use of iron and glass, to create a spacious, well illuminated covered area. The slender columns supporting the roof are spaced out delicately along the platforms; altogether a most elegant concept. Note the complete rakes of clerestory roofed carriages.

59, *bottom*. The interior of Kings Cross, showing the iron and glass roof which replaced an earlier wooden structure of similar dimensions.

to turn the clock back and replace the diesel locomotives of today with their steam predecessors. The true vision must be one of columns of steam cascading high into the ironwork above, with slanting rays of sunlight breaking through, and all about us the echoes of a busy railway station. Today Paddington is impressive still—but cold. An architectural monument to the steam age which seems altogether too grand for the austere demands of internal combustion !

Two other London termini constructed during the period, and still with us today, must surely rank among the great classics of Victorian architecture. By strange chance they stand in close juxtaposition on the Euston Road. I refer of course to Kings Cross and St. Pancras, a most interesting contrast of styles.

60, *above*. Lewis Cubitt's Kings Cross; one of the most powerful visual treatments ever produced for a major terminus. Although it possesses some of the same simple grandeur associated with the great railway viaducts, it was not greatly admired in Victorian times.

61, *right*. A masterpiece of the Gothic revival, St. Pancras station, Midland Railway. This exterior view was taken at 6.45 a.m. on a sunny morning, in 1876.

62, *above.* The great iron roof at St. Pancras, by W. H. Barlow, is in complete contrast to Gilbert Scott's building. Today we can appreciate both as masterpieces in their own right.

63, *left.* The interior of the booking hall at St. Pancras clearly shows the tremendous care in detailing and workmanship. It has more the atmosphere of religion than of workaday transportation.

64, *right.* Brunel's Great Western 7ft. gauge main line had many striking architectural features. This is the portal of a short tunnel between Bristol and Bath, from one of Bourne's lithographs. A 2-2-2 of Daniel Gooch's 'FIREFLY' class is emerging. The top-hatted policeman on the left signals 'all clear' to the driver.

65, *below.* Brunel's famous Box Tunnel, on the Great Western main line. When built, it was the longest and straightest tunnel in the world. Lithograph by J. C. Bourne.

The earlier of the two, Kings Cross (1852) by Lewis Cubitt is a straightforward design with considerable emphasis upon its function as a train shed. The two great arches—arrival and departure—project right through the façade to become a major feature of the design. All the offices are situated to the sides and treated in simple but effective manner. Many Victorians disliked it.

St. Pancras is by way of contrast an example of the strict division of 'office block' and 'train shed'. It is without doubt a masterpiece of mid-Victorian architecture, showing the great diversity of styles, or ideals, then in vogue. For we have the great iron roof, spanning all the tracks without supports, by W. H. Barlow, a wonderful piece of engineering design of functional nature, and in front of this (and butted right against it) is Gilbert Scott's magnificent hotel and station building. The building is the very epitome of the Gothic revival, but one searches in vain for any visual expression of its function as a railway station! Nevertheless it is a magnificent building, with a tremendous skyline and wonderful handling of variegated materials. Quite understandably it was a tremendous attraction when new. Some photographs (now reproduced it is believed, for the first time) were recently unearthed, showing the station when it still had a pristine freshness about its appearance. What an impressive sight it must have been when the Euston Road was still the province of horses and pedestrians.

Besides the great stations, there were the viaducts—in stone, brick, timber and cast iron—carrying the passengers high over valleys, or the chimneys of industrial towns; the bridges, many with beautiful architectural furnishings and of daring new dimensions (such as Brunel's graceful shallow spans across the river at Maidenhead); the tunnel entrances, and numerous specialised buildings *en route*. In this short essay there is hardly room to do justice to so vast a field. What it is important to stress is that, unlike the trains it served, railway architecture reached probably its finest heights of taste and achievement in the period 1830–1870.

66, *above.* A remarkably bold and simple treatment for a tunnel mouth, at Milford on the North Midland Railway. Lithograph by Russell.

67, *below.* Primrose Hill Tunnel, London and Birmingham Railway. A classical treatment which cannot have failed to impress travellers upon the new railway. Lithograph by J. C. Bourne.

Opposite page:

68, *top.* Another Brunel masterpiece. The Wharncliffe Viaduct at Hanwell, executed in the Egyptian style he also favoured for his Clifton Suspension Bridge.

69, *bottom.* Carmichael's engraving of the Wetherall Viaduct. A harmonious blend of architecture and landscape.

This page:

70, *above.* The impressive viaduct at Brighton, carrying the line to Lewes over the London Road. The arches in the left foreground were destroyed by enemy bombs during World War 2, but were carefully rebuilt to the original style. An electric train is crossing the new arches in this 1947 view. The bold grandeur of the viaduct contrasts well with the clutter of houses below.

71, *top.* The intersection bridge, with the
St. Helens and Runcorn Gap Railway crossing
the Liverpool and Manchester Railway. This
rare Ackermann print shows the *Rocket* as
rebuilt, on the left.

72, *lower left.* When occasion arose, bridges
were designed in keeping with their surroundings, sometimes at the request of local land-
owners. This is a bridge at Rugby, London and
Birmingham Railway. Lithographed by Bourne.

73, *lower right.* A straightforward piece of
bridge design, at Blisworth, on the London and
Birmingham Railway. One of Bury's small
locomotives is crossing with a train. Typical of
numerous bridges of comparable size.

74, *above.* Brunel's final masterpiece, the bridge over the River Tamar, at Saltash. This fine view was taken during the Centenary celebrations in 1959, when it was floodlit at night.

75, *left.* Robert Stephenson's Britannia Tubular Bridge, over the Menai Straits. Drawing shows the bridge under construction in 1849.

4 | Ephemera and Uniforms

Liverpool and Manchester
RAIL-WAY.

TIME OF DEPARTURE
BOTH

From Liverpool & Manchester.

FIRST CLASS, FARE 5s.	SECOND CLASS, FARE 3s. 6d.
Seven o'Clock Morning.	Eight o'Clock Morning.
Ten „ Do.	Half-past Two Afternoon.
One „ Afternoon.	
Half-past Four Do.	

• For the convenience of Merchants and others, the First Class evening train of Carriages does not leave Manchester on Tuesdays and Saturdays until Half-past Five o'Clock.

The journey is usually accomplished by the First Class Carriages under two hours.

In addition to the above trains it is intended shortly to add three or four more departures daily.

The Company have commenced carrying GOODS of all kinds on the Rail-way.

January, 1831.

76. Timetable sheet for the Liverpool and Manchester Railway, 1831. Note the hyphenated spelling of Rail-Way.

Two other features of the railway scene which constantly come before the eyes of the public, in addition to its trains and buildings, are the posters it publishes and the uniforms worn by its staff. Both tend to have an element of fashion in their design, typical of their period, and study of these helps us to gain a clearer picture of their respective times.

A railway must publicise its services, by means of posters, handbills and timetable sheets. The majority of such printed matter comes under the heading of *ephemera*; i.e., to be thrown away once it has served its purpose. Fortunately for us there have always been collectors of such items and a good selection of early railway printed matter has survived to the present day. A few carefully selected examples are reproduced in this book to give a fairly representative picture.

The railways have always been huge users of printed matter; during Victorian days they had considerable influence upon the growth of the printing industry, and also upon advertising.

The design of the earliest printed matter for railways was left very much in the hands of various jobbing printers. They followed the general conventions of the day as seen on theatre and race bills. The printers had a good selection of bold display typefaces which they used alternately on the same item to great effect. Important words, names or dates were emphasised by choice of a suitable character of letterform, and a sort of instinctive good taste seems to have guided the hands of these jobbing printers, who produced many beautiful designs.

One interesting development was the use of decorative line drawings of a steam locomotive hauling a train (usually a 2–2–2 of uncertain build); these were cut by typefounders and widely used by the printers. The same cut could appear on the printed matter of many different railway companies. It was also used on theatre bills and suchlike, to draw attention to announcements concerning the time of the last train home! Regrettably the typefounders overlooked the fact that steam locomotive development was proceeding apace, and they continued to issue the little 2–2–2's long after these had been superseded in reality.

By the year of the Great Exhibition, railway posters and handbills were following a fairly set pattern of design, based upon varied typefaces cleverly used together. Printing in two or three colours added emphasis and appeal, and sometimes coloured paper was used. The Great Northern Railway poster of 1851 (page 58), was printed in three colours, with black used to great effect as a shadow on some letterforms. No great change took place in the following 20 years, but many examples of great beauty were produced, such as the delicate layout announcing an excursion to Blenheim produced by a Worcester printer in 1853.

Uniforms were soon provided for certain grades of railway staff, either to distinguish them for easy recognition, or else to suit them for the job they had to perform. Thus we have the extremes of the dandified ' Policeman ', and the rugged engine driver.

The policeman acted as a hand-signalman at strategic points

LLANELLY & VALE OF TOWY
RAILWAYS.

LLANELLY, LLANDILO, LLANDOVERY & CWMAMMAN

On and after NOVEMBER 15th, 1858.

DISTANCE	UP-TRAINS. STARTING FROM	1, 2 & 3 Class.	1, 2 & 3 Class.	1, 2 & 3 Class.	FARES. 1st Class	2nd Class	3rd Class	DISTANCE	DOWN-TRAINS. STARTING FROM	1, 2 & 3 Class.	1, 2 & 3 Class.	1, 2 & 3 Class.	FARES. 1st Class	2nd Class	3rd Class
	Llanelly	8.40	1.45	5.0					Llandovery	8.55	2.40	6.40			
¼	Dock	8.45	1.50	5.4	0 3	0 2	0 1	3½	Lampeter Road	9.5	2.50	6.50	0 9	0 7	0 5½
3	Bynea	8.50	1.55	5.12	0 9	0 6	0 3	5½	Langadock	9.10	2.55	6.55	1 2	0 11	0 6½
6½	Llangennech	8.55	2.0	5.18	1 0	0 8	0 5	7½	Glanrhyd	9.15	3.0	7.0	1 6	1 2	0 7
7½	Pontardulais	9.5	2.10	5.25	1 6	1 2	0 7	11	Llandilo	9.25	3.5	7.10	2 3	1 9	0 11
	*Garnant depart.	8.50		5.10				12	Fairfach	9.30	3.10	7.15	3 6	1 11	1 0
	Cross-Inn	9.10		5.35				14½	Derwydd Road	9.40	3.90	7.95	2 10	2 3	1 3½
13	Cross-Inn arrive.	10.0		5.50	2 6	1 10	1 1	16	Llandebie	9.45	3.30	7.30	3 6	2 6	1 4
17	*Garnant	10.25		6.15	3 3	2 3	1 5		*Garnant depart.	8.50		7.0			
15	Llandebie	9.30	2.35	5.50	3 3	2 3	1 3		Cross-Inn	9.10		7.25			
18½	Derwydd Road	9.40	2.45	5.55	3 6	2 7	1 4½	20	Cross-Inn arrive.	10.0		7.40	4 5	3 3	1 8
19	Fairfach	9.50	2.55	6.5	4 0	3 0	1 7	24½	*Garnant	10.25		8.5	4 9	3 8	2 0
20	Llandilo	9.55	3.0	6.10	4 0	3 0	1 8	24	Pontardulais	10.15	3.55	7.55	4 9	3 6	2 0
24	Glanrhyd	10.5	3.10	6.20	4 9	3 7	2 0	26½	Llangennech	10.22	4.2	8.2	5 3	4 0	2 2
25½	Llangadock	10.10	3.15	6.25	5 2	4 0	2 1½	28	Bynea	10.28	4.8	8.8	5 6	4 2	2 4
27½	Lampeter Road	10.15	3.20	6.30	5 6	4 3	2 3½	30	Dock	10.36	4.16	8.16	6 0	4 6	2 6½
31½	Llandovery	10.25	3.30	6.40	6 3	4 8	2 7	31	Llanelly	10.40	4.20	8.20	6 3	4 8	2 7

*Garnant Passengers will be set down or taken up at Gellycedrim or Cross Keys, if required.
Cross Inn Passengers by Middle-day Trains will be set down or taken up at Pantyffynon.

†The Trains will stop at Llangennech, Derwydd Road, and Glanrhyd by signal only; Passengers wishing to alight must give notice to the Guard at the next Station of their intention.

REGULATIONS.

Dogs will be charged Sixpence each.

Children under three years, no Charge; above three years and under twelve, at Half-price.

Tickets issued at intermediate Stations are so issued conditionally upon the chance of there being room in the Carriages, on the arrival of the Train, and if there be no room, the money will be returned for any Ticket produced at the Booking Office, immediately after the departure of the Train for which it had been purchased. Tickets must be shown to the Company's Servants, or delivered up to them when demanded. Parties not producing their Tickets are liable to be charged the Fare from the most distant Station from which the Train shall have started---they are only available on the day of issue. Parties cannot re-book at an intermediate Station by the same Train. No Tickets will be issued after a Train is in sight at an intermediate Station.

Return Day Tickets, not Transferable, are issued at a reduction of about one-fourth on the double Journey, to First and Second-Class Passengers. Saturday Tickets will be available on the day of issue, or on the following Monday.

The published Train Bills are only intended to fix the time at which Passengers may obtain their Tickets at the various Stations; it being understood that the Trains will not start from them before the appointed time. Every attention shall be paid to insure punctuality; but the Company Give Notice that they do not undertake that

the Trains shall start or arrive at the time specified in the Bills; nor will they be accountable for any loss, inconvenience, or injury which may arise from delay or detention.

Luggage---First Class Passengers are allowed 100lbs. of Luggage; and Second and Third, 60lbs. of Luggage, Free of Charge, not being merchandize or other articles carried for hire or profit; all excess will be charged for. Passengers are requested to place on each article, their Name and Address; and Notice is Hereby Given that the Company will not be responsible for the care of the same unless booked and paid for accordingly.

Parcels---The Company are not responsible for any Parcel above the Value of £10, unless declared as such at the time of booking, and entered and paid for Insurance at 2½ per cent. upon such declared value. To ensure Parcels being forwarded, they must be delivered at the Booking Offices half an hour before the departure of the Trains.

PARCEL RATES

Incivility---It is requested that any instance of misconduct on the part of the persons employed at the Stations, may be directly reported to the Traffic Manager.

JOHN THOMAS, PRINTER, LLANELLY.

along the route, and he was easily recognised by his top hat, tail coat and tight trousers. The colours of this ensemble varied from railway to railway; another feature was his truncheon. This was decorated with the arms and initials of the company.

The grit-impregnated clothes of the driver and fireman were intended for protection rather than appearance, and the life they led—constantly exposed to the weather, to heat and steam—largely dictated their uniform. This was usually of strong cloth, with perhaps a waistcoat, with a neckerchief worn loose around the neck, and a peaked cap which could be pulled well down over the eyes. The cap might be of a weatherproof oilskin texture. Sturdy boots were desirable and in some districts wooden clogs were favoured (a tradition which has persisted in parts of North West England up to the demise of steam!).

The railway guard became a figure of some dignity and importance, with frequent contact with passengers at stations. By the 'fifties he usually wore an impressive uniform with a large belt and buckle and peaked cap. He must have been quite a swashbuckling figure as he supervised the loading of luggage, or directed elderly maiden ladies to their correct compartment!

77, *above left.* Notice of 1838, by an Aylesbury jobbing printer, with great emphasis placed upon the word railway.

78, *above right.* A classic example of a jobbing printer's instinctive sense of style. The charming little woodcut of a locomotive and train was a stock item and was widely employed irrespective of the railway concerned.

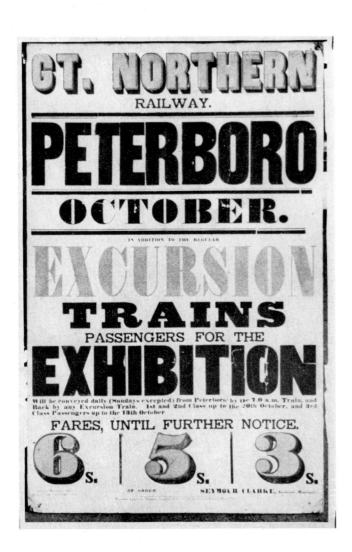

GT. NORTHERN
RAILWAY.

PETERBORO

OCTOBER.

IN ADDITION TO THE REGULAR

EXCURSION

TRAINS

PASSENGERS FOR THE

EXHIBITION

Will be conveyed daily (Sundays excepted) from Peterboro' by the 7.0 a.m. Train, and Back by any Excursion Train. 1st and 2nd Class up to the 20th October, and 3rd Class Passengers up to the 13th October

FARES, UNTIL FURTHER NOTICE.

6s. 5s. 3s.

BY ORDER SEYMOUR CLARKE, General Manager.

OXFORD, WORCESTER, AND WOLVERHAMPTON RAILWAY.

EXCURSION

At Reduced Fares,

FROM EVESHAM

TO

BLENHEIM,

THE

SEAT OF THE DUKE OF MARLBOROUGH.

ON WEDNESDAY NEXT, THE 22ND JUNE,

Tickets, at Reduced Fares, will be issued by the Train leaving Worcester at 7 30 a.m., Returning from the Handborough Station (within 2 Miles of Blenheim) at 6 50 p.m. A number of Conveyances will pe provided at the Station.

An early application for Tickets should be made as only a limited number will be issued.

Fares to Handborough and Back:

FIRST CLASS   SECOND CLASS

6s. 6d.   4s. 6d.

By Order, W. T. ADCOCK.

JUNE 16TH, 1853.

Printed by J. Stanley, Sidbury Place and Wyld's Lane, Worcester.

This page:

79, *above left.* By 1851 railways were making extensive use of printed handbills and posters to attract custom. This beautiful example was printed in three colours, with black used for the shaded effects. A bold and completely successful use of varied typefaces. **80,** *above right.* A delicate layout, with nice decorative typeface used for the name *Blenheim,* which contrasts well with the weighty emphasis placed upon the word *Excursion.* Handbill of 1853 by a Worcester printer.

81, *near right.* The railway 'policeman', who acted as signalman. Illustrated is a policeman on the Brighton Railway, in typical uniform.

82, *far right.* The passenger train guard became a figure of some importance. His handsome uniform is shown in this etching of an L.N.W.R. guard of 1852, from 'Fore's Contrasts' by H. Alken.

Opposite page:

83. Driver and fireman of L.N.W.R. 'SMALL BLOOMER' No. 103 (see plate 23). The gentleman in the top hat was Mr. Widdowson, pay clerk between London, Stafford and branches, c. 1860-1870.

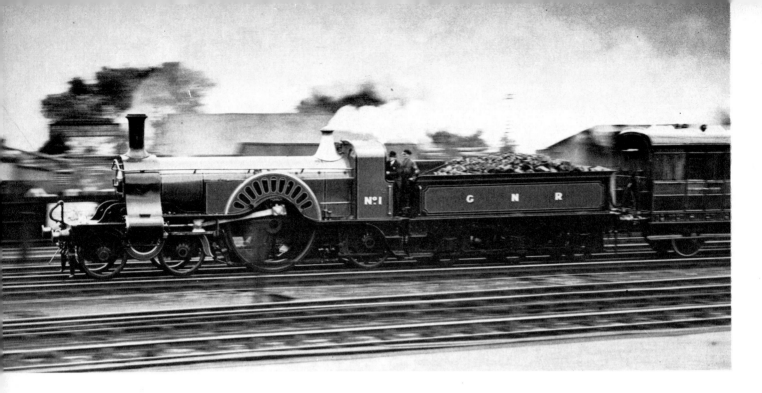

84, *above.* Patrick Stirling's masterpiece. G.N.R. No. 1, shown hauling a special train passing Wood Green. June 30, 1938. Now preserved in York Railway Museum (see also *frontispiece* which depicts a close-up of the driving wheel).

85, *below.* Stroudley single No. 332 *Shanklin,* London, Brighton and South Coast Railway, photographed at Battersea.

Part Two: 1870-1914 The Golden Age of Steam

5 | The Artist Engineers

The first of Patrick Stirling's 8-foot singles, GNR No. 1, steamed out of Doncaster Works in April, 1870. This was to prove one of the classic steam locomotives of all time, with a combination of grace, symmetry and power which won the hearts of countless admirers. It was a victory for aesthetics, for in fact the 8-foot singles were in some ways not the most successful of Stirling's single designs, but they were without doubt the most aristocratic of their breed. The combination of outside cylinders, large driving wheel and flowing curves to frames and footplating, produced a wonderful harmony which looked good whether seen travelling at a mile-a-minute, or standing at rest.

A well-known story which reveals Stirling's jealous appreciation of the good looks of his 8-footers, concerns David Joy (of *Jenny Lind* fame), who produced a drawing showing his valve gear adapted for a Stirling 8-foot single. Stirling would have none of it, dismissing Joy with the words:

' Naa, mon, I canna spile my grand engine with the likes o' that machinery outside o' her.'

Stirling was probably very aware of the fact that the British public had become locomotive ' conscious '. They had started to exhibit signs of that strange love for steam engines which is now hailed as one of our national characteristics—and which to this day remains quite incomprehensible to many foreigners! There was now keen interest in both appearance and performance, and rivalry for the popularity stakes was springing-up between the various companies.

Two other engineers besides Patrick Stirling, were beginning to show their considerable artistic powers at about this time, one was Samuel Waite Johnson; the other, William Stroudley.

Stroudley must be singled-out for the profound effect he had upon locomotive aesthetics during and after his lifetime. From 1865 till 1870 he had been chief locomotive superintendent of the newly formed Highland Railway. Earlier in his career he had worked under Gooch at Swindon, and under Johnson at Glasgow. Whilst on the Highland Railway, Stroudley seems to have been content to rebuild existing locomotives, until 1869, when he produced a very small design of tank engine. But at the end of that year he was appointed Locomotive and Carriage Superintendent of the London Brighton and South Coast Railway, and moved to that company's works at Brighton. The scene that greeted him there was a sorry story of poor discipline, poor maintenance, and (worse still) poor locomotives. His predecessor, John Chester Craven, seems to have taken it upon himself to supply the railway with an immensely varied collection of engines, with hardly any two alike!

The way in which Stroudley ' cleaned-up ' at Brighton has been often retold. He created new discipline and won great respect for himself among the men. Stroudley was a perfectionist, everything had to be ' right ', and he thought each problem out from scratch for himself. He allowed no latitude to his contractors, who had to follow his designs

86. Stroudley's tank engines were every bit as elegant in design and finish as his passenger tender engines. Illustrated *above* is No. 239 *Patcham,* of class 'D1'.

exactly as he wished. It was this love of perfection which outwardly manifested itself in the beautiful series of designs he was to produce for the Brighton line, up to his untimely death in 1889. It was probably also this love of perfection which drove him to launch a terrific onslaught upon the great variety of engines Craven had left him to look after. In this action he must have recalled his early contact with Daniel Gooch, for Stroudley too, was quick to realise the virtues of standardisation, just as Gooch had done when confronted with the varied freaks first produced for the GWR.

In 1872, Stroudley produced a new small tank engine design which he intended primarily to work trains on the South London line. Their snappy performance and small size, soon won them the lasting nickname of *Terriers*. This diminutive design was destined to have one of the most remarkable careers of any steam locomotive ever produced. It was so soundly engineered that it still refuses to die! There are Stroudley *Terriers* in steam today hauling passengers over the private lines of preservation societies, whilst several examples are preserved as museum pieces, including one in Canada. A colour plate, showing how attractive they looked when new, is reproduced on page 108.

The *Terriers* were the smallest of Stroudley's standard tank engines, and yet probably the best loved! For express passenger work the earliest engines Stroudley produced for the Brighton company were some outside framed 2–4–0's and a 2–2–2, which contained parts from certain of Craven's engines. The first 'pure' Stroudley express design was a 2–2–2 single, with 6ft 9in driving wheels, built in 1874. In producing a single, Stroudley chose not to follow the general swing away from single-wheelers which was by then evident. In fact, only two railways continued the regular construction of singles between 1870–1875, these were the Great Northern and the Great Western. The Great Northern singles of the 8-foot design referred to at the beginning of this chapter were introduced very slowly, and only 12 were in service by 1875. Construction of 2–4–0 engines was in some favour, and a notable series was the 800 class produced by Matthew Kirtley for the Midland Railway in 1870.

Whilst most railways were showing a preference for the 2–4–0, and in some cases beginning to consider the virtues of a bogie express

87, *below*. The superb 0-4-2 passenger engines designed by Stroudley had few rivals for quality of workmanship and finish in their day. Class B, No. 215 *Salisbury* is posed in the shed yard at Brighton; in spotless condition.

88, *opposite page*. Drummond 4-4-0 No. 17 of the Caledonian Railway. This superb photograph clearly shows the neatness and simplicity of design, which characterised both Stroudley and Drummond locomotives. The driver, Mr. Soutar, was something of a popular hero of his day.

89. Drummond 4-4-0 No. 79, *Carbrook*, posed outside Carlisle Citadel station. A study in sheer artistry.

engine, Stroudley defied popular opinion and applied front-coupled driving wheels and a trailing carrying wheel to express passenger engines. His most famous examples being undoubtedly the 0–4–2 *Gladstone* class which first appeared in 1882, and we are fortunate that *Gladstone* herself has been preserved at York Museum.

The essence of a Stroudley design was simplicity, impeccable workmanship and beautiful detailing. This was given added distinction by one of the most beautiful copper-capped chimneys ever produced (incidentally the cap itself is very reminiscent of Daniel Gooch's much larger Broad Gauge chimney caps), with a subtle taper to the chimney proper. The dome was simple in shape, with the Salter safety valves incorporated with the minimum of fuss. A most distinctive feature of Stroudley's engines was the cab design, with broad side sheets and a domed roof. But above all it was the detailing and finish which made a Stroudley design a masterpiece of engineering art. Everything, down to the whistle and the numberplate, was treated with the same sense of tasteful restraint. But lest one should imagine such restraint would produce visual boredom, the complete locomotive was finished in one of the most elaborate colour schemes ever bestowed upon steam. Elaborate yes, but certainly not vulgar! It was a wonderful combination of golden ochre, olive green and claret red, set-off to perfection by rich ' lining-out '. But this is anticipating; a later chapter deals with this more fully.

Stroudley's sense of style and discipline in design won countless admirers and his locomotives were a constant source of inspiration to early railway photographers. Hundreds of photographs still exist of his engines, taken by Stroudley devotees in the days when a camera was a most cumbersome piece of equipment to manage.

His influence can be clearly seen in the designs of some of the men who were associated with him at some period in their career. Of these we should list first Dugald Drummond. He had been foreman erector under Stroudley at the Highland Railway's Inverness Works, and he moved to Brighton to become works manager there until 1875. From there he took many Stroudley features to the North British Railway, including a preference for standardisation. His first two engines were virtually copies of the first Stroudley single, and he even used Stroudley's superb livery style! However he avoided the copper-capped chimney, substituting his own plainer, but well proportioned, design. But quite soon Dugald Drummond began to show that he was capable of far more than mere pastiche. He accepted the idea of placing a bogie beneath a locomotive—which Stroudley had certainly not considered desirable—and by 1876 he had produced the first of 12 four-coupled bogie express engines; nevertheless the Stroudley influence remained strongly apparent in the neat simple lines of these engines.

From this batch of North British 4–4–0's we can trace a whole family tree of magnificent 4–4–0 designs, for a number of railways, built by his brother Peter, by his successors on the North British— Mathew Holmes and W. P. Reid—by Lambie and McIntosh on the Caledonian; as well as by himself.

Dugald Drummond moved on from the North British to the neighbouring Caledonian Railway in 1882, taking with him his characteristic style. Thus the Stroudley influence was gradually spreading, so to continue until the first decade of the twentieth century, when Drummond was producing locomotives for the London and South Western Railway, where he had been in power since 1895.

Features of a Drummond engine, and of those inspired by him, were the great simplicity of line and neat finish. Their graceful aspect was enhanced by the flowing line of the 'wing-plates' to the smokebox, by the neat simple splashers (often with combined sandbox on the leading driving wheel splasher), by the *Stroudleyesque* cab, and the beautifully matched straight running plate of both engine and tender. A further point was the balance created by making the centre line of the chimney and the centre line of the bogie one and the same. The engine seemed to be poised upon the rails.

Samuel Waite Johnson, another engineer who possessed a fine aesthetic sense, had worked with David Joy on the drawings for *Jenny Lind* as a young apprentice. By 1870 Johnson was in charge of the Locomotive Department of the Great Eastern Railway and he was beginning to show his ideas on locomotive appearance. He produced his first express engines with bogies, two 4–4–0's, and also some bogie tank engines of 0–4–4T design. These, which had side tanks and inside frames, were to be perpetuated by Johnson, and others, for years to come. But perhaps the most interesting of his designs for the Great Eastern, speaking artistically, was the rebuilding of two of Sinclair's little 2–2–2 singles as 4–2–2's. Sinclair's engine originally had many *Crewe Type* features; Johnson gave them quite an elegant new look, and painted them a bright yellow—perhaps mindful of Stroudley's LBSCR golden ochre scheme.

90. Johnson's rebuild of a Sinclair 2-2-2, as a 4-2-2, for the Great Eastern Railway.

Before his first 4–4–0 was in service on the Great Eastern, Johnson moved to Derby to take over from Matthew Kirtley on the Midland Railway in 1873. Here he found wonderful scope for his powers and he continued with the Midland Railway for the next 30 years or so.

At the time of his arrival on the Midland, a considerable effort was being made by that company to improve the passenger carriages (see Chapter Six), and consequently there was a need for more powerful engines to haul the heavier trains. First of all he produced some 2–4–0's, but in 1876 he repeated the bogie 4–4–0 design he had introduced on

91. A Kirtley 2-4-0, as rebuilt by Johnson; Midland Railway. No. 817.

the Great Eastern; first with 6ft 7in wheels and then a series with 7ft wheels, following with some more engines of the 2–4–0 type.

The true Johnson style is seen on all these Derby engines, and in terms of constructional quality they ranked second to none, except possibly those of Stroudley. The Johnson engines were full of subtle flowing curves. Each part of the locomotive seemed to merge imperceptibly into the whole; there were no awkward corners or angles. The chimney was a masterpiece and the base met the radius of the smokebox so beautifully that it seemed to *grow out* of the engine, rather than to have been placed upon it. The same can be said for the dome cover and the polished brass safety valve cover over the firebox (this had some similarity to the safety valve cover used by Patrick Stirling). A Johnson locomotive was a work of art, and when he decided to change the livery from the green of the Kirtley regime to a deep crimson lake, he added the crowning touch to his shapely designs.

Locomotive development in general was progressing steadily, with larger engines being requested to pull heavier trains. Cabs were becoming a feature of new designs, in place of the previous weatherboards and side sheets, although not all the cabs were particularly effective. C. Hamilton Ellis, in his book, ' Twenty Locomotive Men ', says of the Johnson cab that it was : ' a pretty little thing, with beautiful curves, and roofs just long enough to send drips down the necks of the enginemen in wet weather '. But if this is a valid criticism of Johnson's cab design, those of Stroudley, Jones, the Drummonds, Stirling and many others, were by now noble affairs and very well thought out from the enginemen's viewpoint.

On the Highland Railway, with the departure of Stroudley to Brighton (and with Dugald Drummond soon following), David Jones took over responsibility. In 1873 he rebuilt one of the *Crewe Type* 2–4–0 goods engines as a bogie engine, and in due course his first express engine design appeared; a 4–4–0 with *Crewe Type* front end framing. But this design showed that Jones had learned a lot from Stroudley (and perhaps Drummond) and there were many *Stroudleyesque* features to these distinctive engines; thereby producing a very interesting marriage of styles! Jones used a neat, roomy, cab design derived from Stroudley and in addition he placed a distinctive new style of chimney upon his engines. This had a double casing; the outer one being provided with louvres in front to increase the draught under certain running conditions.

Chimney design in general was becoming more and more

92. The classic Johnson style is well shown in this photograph of 4-4-0 No. 1343 of the Midland Railway.

93, *left.* David Jones rebuilt a *Crewe Type* 2-4-0, as a bogie engine, No. 7 of the Highland Railway. In due course his own 4-4-0 design appeared, illustrated **94**, *below,* is Highland Railway No. 4 *Ardross*.

attractive. We have seen the shapely chimneys which were the recognised hallmarks of a Stroudley, a Johnson, a Drummond or a Jones design. But there was an alternative convention which although very plain, nevertheless possessed a real dignity; I refer to the so-called 'stove-pipe'. This as its name implies, was utterly straightforward, with no embellishments such as copper, or other, type of cap; yet somehow it was ideally suited to some locomotives. Could a Stroudley engine, or a Johnson, have carried a stove-pipe? It seems sacrilegious to even suggest such an outrage! But Williams Adams put a stove-pipe on many classic designs, including his lovely series of 4—4—0's for the London and South Western Railway. When, at a later date, some of these had their Adams stove-pipe replaced by a Drummond style chimney, some of their character was lost.

Stove-pipe chimneys had been a feature of Robert Sinclair's locomotives, and they were afterwards copied by Connor and Brittain on the Caledonian Railways and by Adams, Massey Bromley, T. W. Worsdell and Holden on the Great Eastern. Although Adams is best remembered for his stove-pipe design, his early locomotives for the North London Railway had a copper-capped chimney rather after the style of Beyer Peacock. When he moved to the Great Eastern Railway (following Johnson's move to Derby) he stopped the change-over from stove-pipes to the Johnson style and reverted to stove-pipes for his own locomotive designs for that railway. In 1878 he moved again, this time to Nine Elms on the London and South Western and the stove-pipe went with him. (Curiously, W. G. Beattie produced some engines for the LSWR, with stove-pipes shortly before Adams succeeded him at Nine Elms.)

There were, of course, railway companies and engineers who remained outwardly unmoved by the productions of the men so far discussed in this chapter. Of these the London and North Western

95, *top*. Broad Gauge 4-2-2, *Inkermann,* final version of the original Gooch design, by Dean.

96, *centre*. Dean produced some convertible engines, illustrated is 2-2-2 No. 3026.

97, *below.* Webb compound No. 1104 *Sunbeam;* London & North Western Railway, 1884.

Railway at Crewe Works comes most readily to mind. And here I will no doubt irritate devotees of that remarkable railway, when I say that a Crewe engine paid scant respect to appearances! Don't misunderstand me—there were plenty of handsome engines produced at Crewe—but no money was spent on adornment. If Midland engines were glowing crimson lake; Brighton engines were golden ochre; Caledonian engines deep blue, those of the self-styled 'Premier Line' were black—by order of the General Manager. A Crewe design was thoroughly workmanlike, with very simple robust construction. Things were bolted together, and one *saw* the bolts! No such nonsense was to be tolerated as copper-capped chimneys or smokebox wingplates; almost the sole concession to sentimentality was a neat brass nameplate on the splasher—but how that brasswork shone, and what lovely names they carried!

Another railway that followed very much its own course in locomotive design in the latter part of the nineteenth century was the Great Western. Here we must pause briefly to pay a further tribute to Daniel Gooch. We encountered this remarkable young man in Chapter One, when, just 'coming of age', he took responsibility for the locomotives of the Great Western Railway. He remained with the company, growing in stature as the years passed. He drove personally the locomotive used on the first train journey made by Queen Victoria; he had the intimate confidence of that great man, I. K. Brunel; but above all he put the locomotive stock of the company into first class order.

When William Dean took command at Swindon (after a period when Joseph Armstrong held office) he continued to build express engines of Gooch type for the Broad Gauge. The writing was on the wall for the 7ft railway, but it took a long time for it to finally die. Meanwhile the locomotives were getting old, and replacements were needed. It was not economical to design new ones, so for the time being Dean was content to perpetuate Gooch's designs. However, Dean later realised the possibilities of building convertible engines, (i.e. engines which would run as Broad Gauge types until the conversion of the gauge to 4ft 8½in, whereupon they would be capable of easy conversion to run on the narrower tracks). It would be true to say that some of these 'convertibles' were visually the most ungainly locomotives ever produced—but what a transformation occurred when they were converted! But this anticipates our story; we must first retrace our steps a few years.

By 1880 bogie locomotives were being produced in increasing numbers, although some engineers still did not favour them. A notable innovation of 1878 was the first ' Mogul ' (2–6–0 wheel arrangement), introduced by the Great Eastern Railway to designs by Adams shortly before he left for the London and South Western Railway. The final design was modified in a number of details by his successor, Massey Bromley, and contained certain American features. Between 1880 and 1889 there was considerable pressure upon engineers to economise, and many experiments were tried to achieve this end, including the principle of compounding. In fact, Webb on the London and North Western Railway had converted a 2–2–2 to compounding in 1879, and by 1882 Crewe Works was producing three-cylinder compound engines. Four classes of express engine were built at Crewe from 1882–1890, known as the *Experiment* (one engine only), *Compound*, *Dreadnought* and *Teutonic* classes, and there were also some compound tank engines. In appearance, Webb's compound experiments followed typical Crewe practice. In fact the tradition set by Webb for locomotive appearance was to remain with the London and North Western for the rest of its separate existence.

In 1884 T. W. Worsdell introduced a compound 4–4–0 for the Great Eastern Railway. This had a large continuous splasher over the two driving wheels, but the design of cab, boiler and details (including the stove-pipe chimney) showed considerable Adams' influence. Worsdell moved from the Great Eastern to the North Eastern, and in 1887 he produced a series of compound 4–4–0's, in which considerably more of his own personality was apparent. The continuous splasher was retained, but now there was a handsome side-window cab and new boiler mountings, including a lovely polished brass safety valve casing, and a shapely chimney casting.

With the invention of steam sanding apparatus in 1886 there was a return to favour for the single driver express passenger locomotive, although construction of 2–4–0 and 4–4–0 types was also continued. The steam sanding proved an effective answer to the wheel-slip problem which had bedevilled single drivers when starting away with

98. T. W. Worsdell's compound 4-4-0 No. 779 of the North Eastern, photographed at Edinburgh Waverley. A spacious cab, and single continuous splasher were features of this elegant design.

99. Perhaps the most graceful of all S. W. Johnson's designs were his single-wheelers. No. 1871 clearly illustrates the subtle flowing lines which were a hallmark of his engines. (See also plate 189).

a train. A handsome bogie single was built in 1886 by Neilson and Company, and exhibited at an Edinburgh Exhibition, afterwards being purchased by the Caledonian Railway, with whom it became number 123. This had a number of obviously Drummond features (plus an Adams' bogie) but it is in doubt just how much Drummond actually had to do with the overall design. No further engines of the class were built, but No. 123 seems to have been a very popular engine, achieving some fame in the famous 'races to the north' in 1888, and today she is happily preserved in Glasgow Transport Museum. A fond memory I recall was to witness her travelling at well over a mile-a-minute, when hauling an enthusiasts' excursion a few years ago. The big single driving wheel seemed to move the train effortlessly, with a special sort of grace.

S. W. Johnson produced a new series of singles for the Midland Railway from 1887, of which there were several varieties, with 4–2–2 wheel arrangement and inside cylinders. These Midland singles had superbly graceful lines. A new pattern of smokebox door made this feature flush with the boiler cleading plates, and a new chimney was used. This was a smooth casting, but retained the familiar Johnson lines

100. An 'ugly duckling' transformed! Dean's 4-2-2 *Wigmore Castle,* G.W.R. No. 3021. Note the huge polished brass dome cover.

of the old built-up pattern. It became the new standard Midland chimney. Brasswork, highly polished of course, was used to great effect by Johnson. Never overdone, it was applied to the splasher rims, axleboxes, whistles, number and safety valve casing. Few locomotives have rivalled these Midland singles for sheer beauty of line and perfection of finish.

Johnson's series of bogie singles culminated in the truly magnificent *Princess of Wales,* which appeared from Derby in 1899. Whilst she possessed the same classic outline as her predecessors, she was a massive engine, and as if to emphasise this Johnson placed a bogie eight-wheel tender behind her. The first of the class, No. 2601 *Princess of Wales,* was exhibited at the Paris exhibition of 1900 (11 years earlier one of her smaller sisters had also been exhibited in Paris). A colour plate reproduced on page 112 shows the classic lines of No. 2601 ; the largest single design to run on a British railway.

Mention has already been made of Dean's ' convertibles '. Some of his 2–2–2 singles began life as convertible engines, with the wheels outside both sets of frames. When converted to 4ft 8½in the wheels went between the double frames, in conventional Stephenson GWR style. History, it is claimed, repeats itself. Certainly this was so with the Great Western 2–2–2's. Just as Gooch's *Great Western* had proved to be nose-end heavy and had eventually been rebuilt as a 4–2–2 following a derailment (see Chapter One), so also did Dean's 2–2–2 design prove troublesome. One of the class, *Wigmore Castle,* broke her leading axle whilst hauling a train through Box Tunnel. As a result the class was rebuilt to bogie 4–2–2 arrangement, and the following 3031 class featured the same bogie. These were indeed ' ugly ducklings ' transformed ; many enthusiasts rated them second to none in terms of locomotive aesthetics.

The Dean bogie singles were certainly an arresting sight, with glittering polished brass, copper and steel. The very large brass dome cover was kept in a highly polished state, and tradition has it that after it had been polished at the sheds, a sack was placed over it to keep it from sooty smuts. When the time came for the locomotive to ' back-down ' from the sheds to the station to couple on to its train, the sack was removed to reveal a glittering brass dome which was guaranteed to impress the passengers !

An interesting comparison can be made between the Dean singles and James Holden's 10 GER 4–2–2's which appeared in 1898. These were the first Holden engines to have a bogie. Hitherto he had built a series of smart little 2–2–2's and 2–4–0's, with quite pronounced Adams' characteristics. But when he turned his attention to producing a single,

101. A mixture of Dean and Johnson influence is to be seen in James Holden's Great Eastern Railway 4-2-2's. No. 11 is illustrated *top of page*. There was considerable family resemblance between **102**, *below left,* the Holden Great Eastern Railway 2-4-0's and their 0-4-2 counterparts by Adams, for the London and South Western Railway. **103**, *below right.*

104. Perhaps the most graceful of Webb's compound designs for the London and North Western Railway was his 'GREATER BRITAIN' class. Illustrated is No. 2054 *Queen Empress,* which was exhibited at Chicago in 1893. She is seen here in special white and purple livery to commemorate Queen Victoria's Jubilee.

105, *below.* Adams produced two series of classic 4-4-0's for the London and South Western Railway; this is No. 580. The leading bogie had a wheelbase of 7ft. 6ins. The plain stovepipe chimney suited them admirably.

the Dean influence was unmistakable; so also was that of Johnson! These GER singles were a strange mixture of styles, but nevertheless they had a certain elegance. The chimney, which was virtually pure Dean, was a departure from the stove-pipe Holden had perpetuated until then.

On the London and North Western Railway, Webb persisted with his efforts at compounding, despite their very mixed performances on the line. A larger eight-wheeled class appeared between 1891 and 1894, known as the *Greater Britain* class, and one of these, the *Queen Empress,* was exhibited at the Chicago Exhibition of 1893. With a very long boiler, they had quite a racy aspect which their performance—alas—did not always live up to. Webb produced further compound designs, and amongst these, his *Black Prince* class of 1897–1900, a bogie 4–4–0, was a smart, well proportioned, design.

The period 1890–1900 saw the production of a whole series of classic 4–4–0 types; of these we can only single out a few for mention in this brief essay. Those of Adams for the London and South Western Railway had the longest bogie wheelbase in the country, 7ft 6in, and it was this feature which gave them an especially handsome outline. There were two series, one with larger driving wheels, but basically very similar in appearance. The big sweep of the frames at the front end; the flowing curves of the splashers and the plain but dignified boiler mountings all added up to a finely balanced, harmonious ensemble; one of the all-time classics from the golden age of steam. Other handsome 4–4–0's were produced by Aspinall for the Lancashire and Yorkshire, and by Worsdell for the North Eastern. On the Caledonian, J. F. McIntosh

106, *above.* Three McIntosh 'DUNALASTAIR'
4-4-0's of the Caledonian Railway, on Royal
Train Pilot duties. These were derived from
Drummond's designs; likewise the North
British 4-4-0 design; **107**, *left,* shows
No. 258 *Glen Roy.*
R. J. Billinton brought some Derby influence to
Brighton. His 4-4-0 designs were graceful
engines and must have looked well in Stroudley's
ochre livery. **108**, *below,* shows No. 316
Goldsmid whilst **109**, *bottom,* shows the larger
boilered type, No. 50 *Tasmania.*

produced the first of his *Dunalastair* class in 1896, in which the Drummond influence was most marked. He put a larger boiler on a basically
Drummond engine, and later series of *Dunalastairs* had progressively
larger boilers still. These engines retained the simple neat lines of
Drummond, and the North British Railway also produced some handsome 4-4-0's of Drummond inspiration.

Mention should also be made of the 4–4–0's designed by
R. J. Billinton for the London Brighton and South Coast Railway, in
which considerable Johnson influence was apparent. The first series,
known as the *Grasshoppers*, comprised graceful, slender-looking
engines, but were sadly under-boilered. The later B4 class remedied this
defect whilst retaining much the same elegant aspect. Their Johnson-
inspired curves were further enhanced by application of Stroudley's
golden ochre livery.

Two further 4–4–0 designs of exceptional beauty must be
mentioned. One was H. S. Wainwright's D class for the South Eastern
and Chatham Railway, introduced in 1901. The other was *Claud
Hamilton*, James Holden's masterpiece for the Great Eastern Railway.
Wainwright's design was set-off to perfection by great attention to
appearance of both metalwork and livery. His livery was most elaborate
and expensive to apply (see Chapter Eight) and there was a beautiful
copper-capped chimney and polished brass dome. One of the class is
preserved in Clapham Museum, and to stand alongside this, even in
the cold, quiet, museum atmosphere, is sufficient to recapture much of
the singularly elegant quality of the design.

This page:

110. H. S. Wainwright's beautiful 'D' class 4-4-0 for the South Eastern & Chatham Railway, 1901.

Opposite page:

111, *top.* Highland Railway 'JONES GOODS' 4-6-0, introduced in 1894. An example is preserved at Glasgow.

112, *centre.* The first British 'Atlantic' design, by H. A. Ivatt, for the Great Northern Railway, 1898. No. 990 (later named *Henry Oakley*) is now preserved at York.

113, *bottom.* Lancashire & Yorkshire Railway 4-4-2 design by J. A. F. Aspinall. Nicknamed 'Highfliers', they had inside cylinders and were the largest and most powerful engines in Britain when new.

Holden's *Claud Hamilton* was number 1900 of the Great Eastern Railway. The number was chosen to commemorate the year she was built, when she was shown at the Paris Exhibition, winning the Grand Prix for Holden. The lovely appearance of this engine, in her rich Great Eastern blue, with polished copper-capped chimney and spacious side-window cab, captured many admirers.

These two 4–4–0 designs probably represent the finest examples of a period of British steam locomotive design which placed great emphasis upon external appearance, and upon superb detail. As such, they are the very epitome of 80 years' development in this country, and even by today's sophisticated standards they can be readily judged as fine examples of industrial design. At a time when public taste was still directed towards the picturesque and the fanciful, the British steam locomotive was supreme in establishing acceptable standards for pure machine art. When Holden's *Claud Hamilton* returned from Paris to take an active part in the day-to-day running of the Great Eastern Railway, the noise of the motor car was already making itself heard upon our roads—albeit, as yet, a novelty. Steam locomotives had developed to the degree that we can now consider them classics; motor cars were mere upstarts; but who could foresee the drastic developments of the next 20 years?

Around the turn of the century, there was already a noticeable trend towards still larger engines to pull heavier trains. The ' single revival ' was quickly over (the last single was built in 1901 to H. A. Ivatt's designs for the Great Northern Railway), and the 2–4–0 was now considered somewhat undersized; no more were built after 1903. Development of larger engines of 4–4–2 and 4–6–0 types had begun. The 4–6–0 had been introduced to Britain by David Jones on the Highland Railway, back in 1894, for goods work. The ' Jones Goods ', as it became known, was followed by a large passenger version, the *Castle* class, introduced on the Highland Railway in 1900. The *Castles* were completed by Peter Drummond, and had several typical Drummond

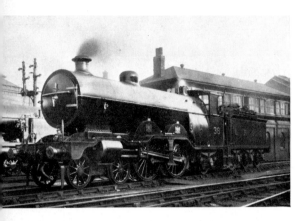

114, *above.* Doncaster influence reached Brighton with the arrival of D. E. Marsh. His Brighton 'Atlantics' had unmistakable Great Northern characteristics. No. 38 of Class HI, is seen in Brighton shed yard.

115, *below.* Most graceful of all the 'Atlantics' were those produced by Robinson for the Great Central Railway. No. 258 is seen in ex-works condition, painted grey for photographic purposes.

features including the chimney and cab. How fascinating all these variations are, when examined in detail. For example, on these two pioneer 4–6–0 designs, both the Jones' and the Drummond cabs had their common origins in Stroudley. Jones used his own louvred chimney; Drummond discarded this in favour of his design, which was closely akin to that of his elder brother. Jones used Stroudley style numberplates on the cab side, with raised numerals; Peter Drummond used brass numberplates with countersunk numerals—and so on. The important fact is that in 1900 the Stroudey influence still persisted in quite a large portion of British locomotive design.

This would seem an opportune moment to review the changes which were about to take place in locomotive aesthetics. We have seen, in such classics as the Johnson and Dean singles, the Holden and Wainwright 4–4–0's, the final essays in late Victorian, early Edwardian, industrial art. This could be summed-up as a nicely proportioned, well balanced machine, with great attention to detail and finish. Now the call was for bigger engines. The loading gauge was dictated by thousands of existing bridges and tunnels. Boilers could be larger, but engines could not be taller. There were also restrictions upon overall width, except on the former broad gauge lines. So by the early years of the twentieth century locomotive engineers were already fully aware of the physical limitations of development they must face. If only Brunel's broad gauge had won acceptance! However, development of the bogie, and of flexible leading and trailing axle designs, permitted engines to be longer, even if they could not be made much wider or taller.

Two schools of thought were apparent in locomotive design in the first decade of the twentieth century. Both schools accepted the need for larger locomotives of greater power, but the actual shape these should take was not so readily agreed. One school, which might be termed 'conventional' (without being in any way derogatory), followed the classic conventions of the 'nineties, producing what were virtually enlarged 4–4–0's, in the shape of 4–4–2's and 4–6–0's. The other

school, which might be referred to as the 'modern' school, evolved a new aestheticism which broke away from existing conventions in many ways.

Early examples of the 'conventional' school of big engines were the two Highland Railway 4–6–0 designs already referred to. In addition to these 4–6–0's there was express engine version produced for the North Eastern Railway by Wilson Worsdell in 1899/1900. But perhaps this period is better described as the era of the 4–4–2 'Atlantic' type. It was the 'Atlantic', an elongated 4–4–0 with an additional carrying axle under the firebox, that won so many hearts for its combination of graceful symmetry and increased power. The first 4–4–2's were by H. A. Ivatt for the Great Northern Railway, and appeared in 1898, starting with the famous 990 *Henry Oakley* (now preserved in York Railway Museum). These had somewhat small boilers for their size. The following year J. A. F. Aspinall produced his famous series of 'Atlantics' for the Lancashire and Yorkshire Railway. Colloquially known as the *Highfliers*, they had inside cylinders, and were the largest and most powerful engines in Britain when new. They had very neat and simple lines, with a great impression of size, emphasised by the high pitch of the boiler and the big splashers housing the 7ft 3in driving wheels.

When Ivatt's *Henry Oakley* was placed in service it caused quite a sensation in that it was unlike any British locomotive then running. But perhaps the large-boilered version he produced in 1903 was even more striking, with a wide firebox giving the onlooker a sense of enormous capacity. Two years later, in 1905, the Great Northern 'Atlantic' design was repeated with only minor differences on the London Brighton and South Coast Railway by D. E. Marsh, who had previously been chief assistant to H. A. Ivatt at Doncaster. What an amazing course of events Brighton had witnessed! First Stroudley's superb engines, then R. J. Billinton bringing some Johnson influence from Derby, now Marsh introducing Ivatt's Doncaster practices. In 1910 a further batch of 'Atlantics' was produced by Marsh but completed by his successor, Lawson Billinton (son of R. J. Billinton) who slightly altered their appearance, in particular smoothing out the curves of the footplating; a distinct improvement.

116. The North British 'Atlantics' had many features in common with the Robinson engines, although the squat chimney altered their outline considerably.

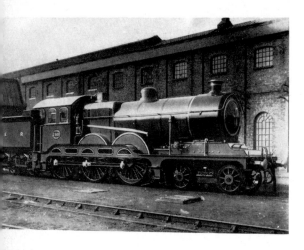

117. Holden's 4-6-0 for the Great Eastern Railway, No. 1500. Note the large cab which encloses the rear driving wheel splasher.

118. The famous Caledonian Railway inside-cylinder 4-6-0 design by McIntosh; the Drummond style carried through successfully to a really large passenger engine. Illustrated is No. 904. Note the large bogie tender.

Two other 'Atlantic' designs of imposing appearance, and with many features in common, were the Robinson locomotives for the Great Central Railway and those ordered from the North British Locomotive Company for the North British Railway. The Robinson engines were built between 1903 and 1906, and many people consider them to be the most handsome engines of their time. They were massive, but beautifully proportioned, and the Robinson pattern of chimney casing was a veritable masterpiece. Except for the horizontal lines of the flange and lip, this chimney (as fitted to the 'Atlantics') did not have a straight line anywhere on its outer surface. How perfectly it matched the curves of the engine, which were subtle yet strong. Engine and tender were beautifully matched, and the tender was distinguished by curved solid coal guards. The N.B.R. 'Atlantics' were constructed between 1906–1911, and it seems that they were produced almost straight from Robinson's design. There is considerable similarity between the two, especially about the frames and running plate. The North British loading gauge was restricted in height, and they were forced to place a squat dome and chimney upon the big boiler of their 'Atlantics'. This gave them an impression of being even larger than they really were.

In addition to his graceful 4–4–2's, Robinson produced a number of well proportioned engines for the Great Central Railway. Of these, we should mention the inside-cylinder 4–6–0 *Sir Sam Fay*, of 1912, and the huge inside-cylinder 4–4–0 *Director* class of 1913. All his designs bore a strong family likeness, and despite the fact that the last two mentioned had inside cylinders, all had a very modern look which resulted from their massive yet elegant dimensions.

On the Great Eastern Railway S. D. Holden produced a 4–6–0 inside-cylinder design in 1911 which was visually an enlarged *Claud Hamilton*. This had a most impressive side-window cab, with side sheets so long that a complete driving wheel splasher was included in them! It is perhaps worthwhile pointing out that at this time certain railways still persisted with cab designs dating from Victorian days, which did not have side windows—notably the LNWR, where Webb's design was continued unchanged.

On the Caledonian Railway, McIntosh continued to build still larger engines, having shown the way with his famous *Dunalastair* series of 4–4–0's. These grew into 4–6–0's, with both passenger and goods versions. Through all his designs there ran the same Drummond inspired simplicity, and even his large 4–6–0 passenger engines (of which the best known and best loved was the fabulous *Cardean* of 1906) had the

same classic treatment, and a feeling of poise and dignity despite their imposing size. At Crewe, George Whale had taken over from Webb in 1903. He was immediately faced with the unenviable task of operating the line with a locomotive stud comprised of, on the one hand, old and undersized but reliable designs, and on the other hand, larger and newer —but incompetent—Webb compounds. Whale set to work to produce a design for a new *simple* 4–4–0, and his well known *Precursor* class appeared from Crewe just nine months after he took office. These went straight into mass production off the drawing board, and were very well received by the enginemen. Whale also designed a 4–6–0, the inside-cylindered *Experiment* class, which was not so well received to begin with, but his successor, Bowen Cooke, improved the design without much alteration to appearance, in his *Prince of Wales* class. He likewise produced a superheated version of Whale's *Precursor* 4–4–0 which was known as the *George the Fifth* class. This had a different driving wheel splasher design and a longer smokebox.

In 1913 Bowen Cooke built the first really big express engine the London and North Western Railway possessed. This was his four-cylinder 4–6–0 No. 2222 *Sir Gilbert Claughton*, a fine looking engine which attracted much attention. Yet even this had the old familiar Crewe 'hallmarks' of chimney and cab design, but she had outside Walschaerts valve gear, and we might justifiably describe her as the LNWR contribution to the 'modern' school of design.

One company that resisted the trend towards bigger engines was the Midland; they never built a six-coupled express engine, or an 'Atlantic' for that matter. But if Derby did not feel inclined to build larger than 4–4–0's, it did attempt to improve their design and performance, and compounding was one outcome of this. Although Webb's efforts at compounding on the London and North Western must have made many engineers fight shy of the idea, a system developed by W. M. Smith on the North Eastern Railway had proved to be considerably more successful. Smith's system was adopted by S. W. Johnson on the Midland Railway in 1901–1903, for five three-cylinder 4–4–0's built at Derby. Johnson retired in 1904 and his successor was Richard Deeley, who had been his works manager. The following year Deeley brought out the first of his modified version of the Smith/Johnson compound, and this was a fine 'racey' looking machine with neat lines marred only by a rather clumsy chimney. Although Deeley also built some simple

119, *above.* Scarcely less elegant than his passenger 4-6-0's were the mixed traffic versions produced by McIntosh for the Caledonian. Class 918, No. 920 is seen here in ex-works condition being 'steamed-up' for the road. Alongside, an elderly outside-cylinder 0-4-2, No. 1627, stands forlorn, with condemned markings.

120, *above.* Four cylinder 4-6-0 No. 1914 *Patriot,* designed by Bowen Cooke for the L.N.W.R. His 'CLAUGHTON'S' may be described as Crewe's contribution to the 'modern' school of design.

4–4–0's of comparable size, the compounds—or ' Crimson Ramblers ' as they became known—proved very successful. We shall encounter them again, in greater detail, in Volume Two.

Briefly then we have examined some of the highlights of the ' conventional ' school of early twentieth century locomotive design. Inevitably many worthy examples have been left out, and we can only acknowledge in passing the contributions of Manson, Worsdell and many others who were also producing beautiful locomotive designs about this time.

The figurehead of the ' modern ' school of locomotive aesthetics was without doubt Swindon. In 1902, G. J. Churchward was appointed to succeed Dean as head at Swindon. Prior to this, in his office as works manager and chief assistant to Dean, he had built the first outside-cylinder 4–6–0 for the Great Western. It is commonly believed that he was basically responsible for the design. This was No. 100 (later named *William Dean*), and it marked the beginning of a completely new aesthetic convention for British express passenger engines. J. N. Maskelyne, in his book ' Locomotives I Have Known ', recalls that when No. 100 appeared, locomotive enthusiasts everywhere were profoundly shocked by her appearance. Certainly the style introduced by Church-ward was completely new to British eyes ; principal features being the domeless boiler with brass safety valve casing ; Belpaire flat-topped firebox ; medium high running plate with small splashers. In her outline we see the precursor of the modern express passenger engines produced by Swindon, and others, for the ensuing 50 years or so. Henceforth Swindon engines were unmistakable, and a proud tradition arose regarding their appearance. The tapered boiler barrel (which appeared on a second 4–6–0, No. 98), polished copper-capped chimney and brass safety valve casing became the hall-marks of Swindon, just as Webb's chimney and cab had done at Crewe.

Churchward experimented with both 4–6–0 and 4–4–2 wheel arrangement to determine which was best for future development, and he even purchased three of the well-known De Glehn compounds from France for comparison. Eventually he decided in favour of the 4–6–0, and some engines which started life as 4–4–2's were rebuilt accordingly. He produced both two-cylinder and four-cylinder designs. The four-

Opposite page:

121, *above left.* Front end of Great Eastern Railway 2-4-0 No. 490 (preserved at Museum of British Transport, Clapham).

122, *above right.* Front end of London Brighton and South Coast Railway Marsh 'Atlantic' No. 40.

123, *below left.* Front end of Midland Railway Compound 4-4-0 No. 1000. (Preserved at Museum of British Transport, Clapham).

124, *below right.* Front end of Great Central Railway 'Director' class 4-4-0 by Robinson. Note that the rivet heads around the smokebox door are a latter day addition. (Preserved at Museum of British Transport, Clapham).

This page:

125, *below.* Midland Railway Compound 4-4-0 No. 1012 at St. Pancras station, on a train of clerestory roofed carriages.

126, *right.* G.W.R. 4-6-0, No. 178 *Kirkland* speeds the 3.30 p.m. express from Paddington. The new look in locomotive design, introduced by J. G. Churchward at Swindon, shocked many enthusiasts at the time. But there was no denying the excellence of his locomotives in service.

cylinder type, known as the *Star* class, was strikingly modern for its time and by far the most successful four-cylinder 4-6-0 built in the period under review. Drummond, on the London and South Western, experimented with four-cylinder 4–6–0's but not with any great success. His engines seemed huge but clumsy and very indifferent performers. Drummond 'saved his face', so to speak, by producing a really fine 4–4–0 design in 1912, of class D15, which may perhaps be considered as his masterpiece. Had Drummond been content to produce a two-cylinder 4–6–0 he might have come up with a winner comparable to McIntosh's *Cardean*! But we digress.

Having shocked the enthusiast world by his new ideas on locomotive lineage, Churchward remained faithful to his ideals. There was his 4–4–0 design, the *County* class of 1904–1911, in which the new lines were very well handled; yet to some eyes at the time they seemed ugly. Perhaps those same eyes were more prepared for the shock when in 1908 Churchward built *The Great Bear,* the first 4–6–2 to run on a British railway. A huge and heavy engine that was ahead of its time in conception, it was nonetheless prophetic. It remained the only 'Pacific' type ever built at Swindon, and the sole example in Britain for 14 years.

By mid-1914, as the threat of war hung heavily in the air, there were many signs of change in the world of locomotive design. Besides

127, *below.* Churchward's solitary 'Pacific', *The Great Bear* of 1908.

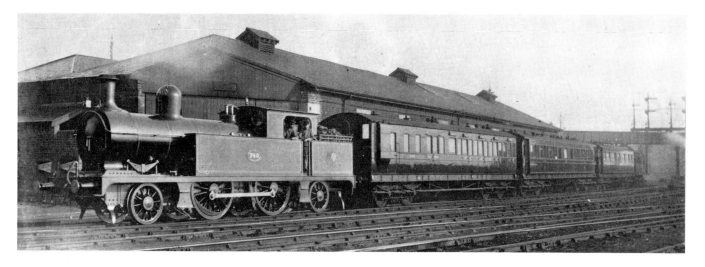

the significant contribution of Churchward on the Great Western, there was the generally increasing use of superheating; of Belpaire fireboxes; outside cylinders and Walschaert's valve gear. On the Great Northern Railway, H. A. Ivatt had been succeeded by Nigel Gresley in 1911, and whilst Gresley was apparently happy to follow Doncaster practice in locomotive appearance to quite a considerable degree, he showed the way future developments would take when he produced a class of mixed-traffic 2–6–0's in 1912–1913. These had outside Walschaert's gear and most significantly, a high running plate over the driving wheels, so high that there were no splashers.

Finally, although we are primarily concerned with the development of express passenger engines in this essay, mention should be briefly made of a few of the fine designs for tank engines and goods engines which appeared in the first decade or so of the twentieth century.

Tank engine designs had progressed to the point where they included types capable of hauling fast main line trains for distances up to about 80 miles. These were mostly six-coupled outside-cylinder engines, but there were also 0–4–4T and 2–4–2T classes which were capable of a good turn of speed when required. The 2–4–2T's of the Lancashire and Yorkshire Railway were used continuously on main line trains and there are accounts of some remarkable runs behind these sprightly engines. The 0–4–4T type was built by Dugald Drummond on the LSWR and Harry Wainwright on the South Eastern and Chatham. Drummond's 0–4–4T's, the M7 class, were built between 1897 and 1911 and were the standard design for LSWR suburban duties. The derivation

128, *above.* The Lancashire and Yorkshire Railway possessed a fleet of sturdy 2-4-2T's which were capable of express passenger performances. They had neat, simple outlines, with nicely balanced proportions.

129, *below.* One of the most attractive tank engine designs must surely have been the Adams 4-4-2T's for the London and South Western Railway. A survivor still operates on the Bluebell Railway.

130, *above.* 'Baltic' tank engine by Lawson Billinton for the L.B.S.C.R.

131, *below.* Churchward's 2-8-0 design Great Western Railway.

132, *bottom.* Robinson's Great Central 2-8-0, which was adopted by the War Department. Illustrated is one operated by the G.W.R., as their No. 3014.

from his earlier engines on the North British and Caledonian was quite obvious, but they were probably the best tank engines he produced. Some examples remained in service in the 1960's and they were still capable of putting up a good performance then. They were graceful engines with a good turn of speed.

Wainwright's 0–4–4T, the H class, was also intended for suburban work. They were very solid, sturdy engines with the same beautiful finish that Wainwright put on his big tender 4–4–0's. Built between 1904 and 1915, quite a number survived until the 1960's, virtually unaltered in appearance. My last memories of the class are of a few stationed at Three Bridges where they worked turn-and-turn-about with some Drummond M7's on the line to East Grinstead. The enginemen preferred the Wainwright design, incidentally.

A four-coupled tank engine design by Douglas Earle Marsh for the London Brighton and South Coast Railway deserves mention for both appearance and performance. Known officially as the I3 class, they had 4–4–2T wheel arrangement and inside cylinders and were built between 1907 and 1913. These were so successful that Marsh was prompted to produce an even larger tank engine for the Brighton company, and in 1910 there duly appeared No. 325 *Abergavenny*. With a 4–6–2 wheel arrangement she was a singularly neat and handsome design; a second engine No. 326 *Bessborough* had the outside Walschaert's valve gear instead of inside Stephenson's gear, but was otherwise similar. To onlookers this pair must have seemed the ultimate word in tank engine design—surely they could not be enlarged upon yet further? But only three years later Brighton produced an even larger and more imposing design. This was by Lawson Billinton, who retained a good deal of the Marsh style. But the newcomer was really massive, and with a 4–6–4 wheel arrangement it ranked as a powerful express engine by any railway's standards. Only two of the class appeared by the end of 1914, but after World War I a further batch of examples (with some modifications) was produced in 1921–1922.

The design of goods locomotives took full advantage of the improvements made to passenger types. Larger boilers, six- and even eight-coupled wheels and greater flexibility of wheelbase, were the order of the day. We have already encountered the Highland Railway *Jones Goods* and the Caledonian Railway McIntosh goods 4–6–0's. Other railways followed suit with similar bogie engines for fast goods work. The 0–6–0 and 0–8–0 were mostly favoured for slow, heavy, mineral trains and suchlike.

There was an interesting development in 1899–1900 when a batch of 80 American bar-framed 2–6–0 'Moguls' were imported, owing to the fact that British builders were so overwhelmed with work that they could not accept more orders. The Midland Railway had 40; the Great Northern, 20; and the Great Central, 20. They were typically American in design (such as were used on light railways in the United States and elsewhere in the World), and very simple in layout. The few concessions to British practice included the design of boiler mountings, which varied according to which railway they were delivered. They do not seem to have been popular with our railwaymen, and none lasted more than 15 or so years (compared with the great age attained by many contemporary British goods engines, this was very short).

The 2–8–0 goods type made its debut in 1903 when Churchward produced a design for the Great Western Railway. Robinson on the Great Central and Gresley on the Great Northern followed suit with designs in 1911 and 1913 respectively. The Robinson design, which had the solid, robust qualities combined with a handsome outline which was typical of his engines, was adopted for war work, and 521 engines were built for the R.O.D. (Railway Operating Department of the War Office) for overseas military service. What more fitting conclusion to the present chapter than this? A classic British steam locomotive shipped overseas to aid the war effort—this was no *ugly* weapon of war!

6 Sumptuous Carriages

In Chapter Two we left the railway passenger feeling rather sorry for himself. Despite some advances in construction, the facilities for comfortable travel were lagging sadly behind the mechanical progress in steam locomotion. True, carriages were longer, wider and slightly higher than those current in the 1850's. But in terms of amenity the second and third class passengers had a raw deal. However, in the period covered in this chapter (1870–1914), railway carriage design underwent marked improvement, and transformation from a still primitive conveyance to an elegant room on wheels.

It was the Midland Railway, in the early 1870's, that took the initiative in improving travelling conditions. The Midland General Manager, James Allport, visited America in 1872 and following this some American-style *Pullman* cars were imported and introduced to British travellers. Despite their superior construction and better riding qualities—not to mention their ornate and lavish comfort—the all-Pullman trains introduced on the Midland did not come up to Allport's expectations, and the complete Pullman trains were disbanded, the cars being used on ordinary trains, together with conventional British stock. Nevertheless they became a status symbol of luxury which has remained synonymous with the name of Pullman in this country to the present day. A supplementary fare was charged for the privilege of travelling by Pullman car; and still is.

More significant than the introduction of the Pullman to Britain, was Allport's decision to abolish second-class travel on his railway, and to give third class passengers a comfortable compartment to ride in, with upholstered padded seats and better lighting and ventilation. Naturally this move, acknowledging as it did the changed social conditions arising from mid-Victorian industrial prosperity and greater freedom of travel, was considered revolutionary. Although other companies were more or less forced to follow suit, they remained obstinate in retaining second class accommodation, whilst making third class travel gradually more tolerable.

The 1870's witnessed a move away from rigid wheelbase four- and six-wheeled stock, towards eight- and even twelve-wheelers. Some eight-wheelers had rigid wheelbases, some had a degree of flexibility on the outer axles, and some possessed bogies proper. These latter

133, *top of page.* Pullman Car No. 8, of the Midland Railway, constructed 1876. **134,** *above.* Engraving of the interior of a Midland Railway Pullman Parlour car.

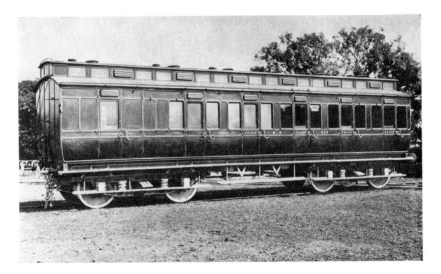

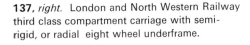

135, *above left.* The new deal for third class passengers. Midland Railway 1875 third class compartment, with stuffed seats and improved lighting and ventilation. (From a mock-up in Clapham Museum).

136, *above right.* Midland Railway bogie clerestory brake third of the 1870's.

137, *right.* London and North Western Railway third class compartment carriage with semi-rigid, or radial eight wheel underframe.

included the American Pullman cars. The twelve-wheeled bogie carriage was pioneered by the Midland and when these appeared they were the longest ordinary passenger carriages in the country, measuring 54ft long over body ends. The Pullman cars were also exceptionally large for their period. Six-wheelers were of course commonplace on trains of the 1870's and pot-oil lamps still provided illumination. Trains were frequently composed of a mixture of carriages, with different lengths and wheel arrangements; some possessing bogies, some not. The bogie allowed greater length of carriage to be safely carried around curves, consequently trains tended to be longer and heavier, making it necessary to produce more powerful locomotives (see previous chapter).

In addition to greater length, the height of carriages was gradually increased. At first this was only by a modest 12in or so, along the centre line of the roof; this was achieved by making the roof an arc-shape. This became possible when luggage was no longer conveyed on the rooftop (a somewhat dangerous practice with hazards such as fire or high winds), and separate luggage compartments, or vans, were provided. The guard also no longer travelled precariously on the rooftop; instead he was positioned in an enclosed elevated 'birdcage' compartment, where he could see over the top of the train. As carriages became yet higher, this 'birdcage' was not always possible within the loading gauge, and an alternative look-out was provided by means of ducket side-windows to the guard's compartment, which was situated within the carriage.

The clerestory roof, (which we have already encountered in Chapter Two, on the Great Western 'Posting Carriages'), now re-appeared on the Great Western and Midland (also on the American-built Pullmans). Besides giving additional headroom, the clerestory provided better natural lighting and ventilation. A drawback was the illumination at night. An oil lamp suspended within the raised clerestory tended to cast heavy shadows to each side of the compart-

ment interior. After a while, the Midland Carriage Superintendent reverted to arc-roofs, but on the Great Western, Dean continued the clerestory. A third and more widespread revival of the clerestory roof was to occur in the 1890's; as we will see presently.

The year 1879 saw the introduction of the first British dining car. Until that date passengers had perforce to either carry their own refreshment in hampers (which could be quite a lavish meal), or else join the throng clamouring to be served during a special stop at one of the station refreshment rooms *en route*. Many stories exist of the profiteering refreshment room managers who purposely produced their beverage or soup so scalding-hot that the luckless passenger could only sip a mouthful or so before the whistle blew, to summon them back to the departing train. Needless to say the remainder of the liquid was duly resold to the next trainload!

At first, dining or refreshment cars were the preserve of the first class passenger. The cars did not possess gangways at each end and it was not yet possible to 'stretch one's legs' and head for the diner whenever the fancy occurred. Either you travelled the whole way in the restaurant car, or else changed carriages at a stop *en route*. The first dining car was, in fact, a Pullman, the *Prince of Wales*, which was specially rebuilt with a kitchen. Later the Great Northern Railway (who operated it) purchased it outright and placed it in ordinary stock.

Sleeping cars of varied concept began to make their appearance, and to begin with the designers seem to have been very uncertain what form they should take. The first proper sleeping carriage was introduced on the North British Railway in 1873, and by 1877 other examples were to be found in use. The most popular early version seems to have been the American Pullman saloon layout, with curtains offering a degree of privacy to each berth. These required passengers to undress whilst on the bed—a complicated manoeuvre for Victorian ladies complete with bustled skirt and tight corsets! The British public, at least those of the wealthier class who could afford to pay for the privacy of a bed on the train, took even more kindly to the idea of having separate compartments to sleep in, linked by a side-corridor. In 1881 the Great Western Railway produced this arrangement in a broad gauge sleeping car which had six two-birth compartments, no fewer than three lavatories, plus a pantry. This carriage was a 'convertible', with narrow body running on broad gauge wheels, to facilitate ease of change-over to the 4ft 8½in system in due course.

Mention should be made here of the improvements made in lighting, heating and brakes for passenger carriages. The Pullman cars had very effective double kerosene lamps with Argand burners (but these were a decided fire risk in a wooden-bodied carriage). They also had oil-fired hot-water heating, a remarkable advance in comfort at a time when the British passenger still froze in cold weather despite his footwarming aids. Lighting on certain railways had changed from the poor pot-oil lamps to coal gas, or compressed oil gas, usually carried in cylinders under the carriage. The compressed oil gas was superior to most systems and it was widely used by British railway companies for many years. A serious disadvantage of gaslighting was the grave fire risk in the event of an accident.

Reverting for a moment to the subject of carriage heating; the footwarmer had been 'improved' by substituting soda-acetate crystals for the use of hot water. The sealed canister of crystals was heated in a mobile vat, and retained the heat for a number of hours. This improvement was first made by the London and North Western Railway, and subsequently adopted elsewhere.

A notable experiment of 1881 was the application of electric lighting to a Pullman car. This was by means of underfloor batteries (Fauré cells) supplying 12 Edison bulbs. Despite their pioneer nature the arrangements worked sufficiently well to encourage William Stroudley to equip four more Pullman cars. Stroudley disliked the heavy battery equipment and replaced this with a generator, driven by

138. Interior of a Pullman sleeping car, Midland Railway.

139. Pullman car *Prince,* of the Brighton line, with enclosed end vestibules and gangways.

an axle, situated in a guard's van, with an accumulator to light the train when stationary. Some 20 or more Brighton trains were equipped with the system as a result of these experiments.

A most important advantage of electric lighting was that it could be turned on or off as required. This at last solved the problem of passing through tunnels during daylight hours. Prior to this such hazards were often negotiated in pitch-black darkness, and both robbery and murder had been committed with the aid of these temporary black-outs. But many years were to pass before electricity replaced gaslighting for British railway carriages. The Pullman company were keen on electric lighting, but until the mid-'nineties their new cars retained alternative means of light in case of failure.

Brakes for passenger trains were the subject of considerable debate. There was much interest in providing continuous brakes, following a number of serious accidents, but it was not clear what form these should take. One method utilised chains; but more sophisticated

140. Interior of a Dean clerestory third class carriage, G.W.R. Note the lack of armrests to the seats, and the huge light pendants.

systems using either a vacuum, or compressed air were soon sought after, as the chains were both cumbersome and difficult to apply smoothly. A series of brake trials took place on the Newark to Nottingham line of the Midland Railway in 1875, with various railway companies competing; these trials involved automatic air-brakes, hydraulic brakes, vacuum brakes and chain brakes. The results favoured the Westinghouse system of air brake, but despite this, many companies chose to go their own way and both vacuum and air brakes were developed. (Could they but have foreseen the events of the 1960's, where British Railways are faced with the reversion to air-brakes despite a fairly recent decision to standardise upon the vacuum brake!)

An aspect of braking dear to the passengers' heart was the emergency communication. A cord system between driver and guard had been recommended by a Select Committee of the House of Commons in 1853, but although this was widely adopted the cord was not supposed to be accessible to the passengers. By 1865 recommendations were made to allow passengers access to the cord, and in 1868 under a Regulation of Railways Act, railway companies were obliged to provide an efficient means of passenger alarm communication on all trains making non-stop runs of 20 miles or more. This usually followed the principle of an outside cord, accessible to passengers through the droplights, and connected either to the engine whistle or to a gong mounted on the side of the tender. Upon hearing the alarm sounded,

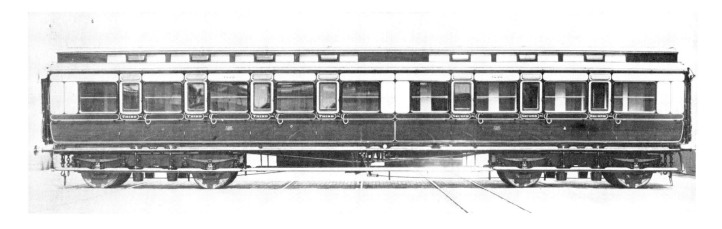

the driver applied the brakes. In 1890 the first move was made towards allowing the passenger to have direct access to the brakes. Approval followed in 1893, and in due course the familiar system of a chain running inside a pipe, with the pipe placed inside the carriage, appeared. Pulling the chain (on dire penalty of a fine for improper use) began applying the brakes on the train. And so it remains in 1968!

Before passing on to what might justifiably be called the 'sumptuous phase' of British passenger carriage design, I would like to mention the external styling of carriages. British carriages followed pretty rigid conventions, stemming (as we have seen in Chapter Two) from road coachbuilding practices. A number of divisions characterised the side of a wooden bodied railway carriage, above and below the waistline. Below the waist, the panelling was usually plain (later some matchboard sides were produced, including Pullman cars); above the waist the side was as a rule subdivided into three 'quarters'—waist-quarter, window-quarter and top-quarter. The waist-quarter panels were horizontal in emphasis and ran along under the windows. These were topped by the windows and adjacent upright panels, above them came the top-quarter panels which were also horizontal and perhaps included ventilator louvres. The actual shape of the panels varied. Some had very rounded corners, others were rectangular with straight mouldings. These conventions in coachbuilding were to remain virtually unchanged until the coming of steel panelled carriages. The typical

141. Clerestory composite second and third class gangwayed carriage, Great Western Railway, 1900.

British carriage still had hinged doors to each compartment. A carriage produced by the Great Northern Railway in 1881 broke away from the existing non-corridor compartment layout and provided a side corridor to each compartment. As such, this (and the similar arrangement on a Great Western sleeping car, already mentioned) represented the prototype of countless hundreds of carriages built ever since with this interior layout. As yet there were no gangways between carriages, but toilet facilities were accessible to passengers within the carriage.

The typical Victorian lavatory carriage, prior to the provision of gangways, remained a non-corridor compartment style vehicle with a lavatory accessible only from immediately adjacent compartments.

It was not until 1891 that the through-corridor train made its appearance, with gangway bellows between carriages. The Great Western produced a complete train of gangwayed side-corridor carriages, and concurrently the Great Eastern provided a dining car train with gangways. Perhaps more important still, the Great Eastern train allowed meals to be served to second and third class passengers. Before long other railways followed suit, with first and third class diners (by now the second class, long abolished by the Midland, was beginning to die out elsewhere). As yet gangwayed corridor trains were by no means universally approved of—the British it seems do not readily alter their habits even when greater comfort is offered—and in some cases only the dining cars were interconnected, with the remainder of the train still comprised of non-corridor stock.

Mention of dining cars brings us to what I have already suggested should be described as the 'sumptuous' phase. (C. Hamilton Ellis also favours this descriptive term, in his book 'British Railway History'.) Sumptuous it indeed was! The late Victorian railway carriage, especially the dining vehicle, had a lavish interior, with rich plush furnishings. To give some idea, take these two contemporary descriptions: the first dated 1897, the second 1899.

From 'The Sketch', August 11th, 1897:

142. Third class dining car, corridor train, introduced by the Midland Railway 1894.

' The Midland Railway new dining-car express trains to Bristol and Bradford are very handsome. The third-class cars have interior fittings of richly coloured and figured mahogany. The seats are upholstered with figured crimson or blue moquette, and shaped so as to give passengers not only a convenient seat while dining, but facility for a comfortable nap after dinner. The roof is panelled with Lincrusta-Walton painted white. The two dining-saloons are connected by the '' kitchen carriage '', a vehicle containing a large kitchen, of adequate size to provide for the dining of 15 first-class and 47 third-class passengers. This kitchen is fitted up with all modern appliances for the preserving and well-cooking of every kind of food required, and attached thereto are a conductor's pantry and stores. In the remainder of the new train the first- and third-class compartments are all constructed in the same superior style, decorated with photographs and mirrors. Ample lavatory accommodation is provided throughout the train.'

The second description comes from the ' Illustrated London News ', July 8th, 1899 :

' NEW MIDLAND CORRIDOR TRAIN
The Midland is again making sweeping changes in the class of carriage which has done duty between St. Pancras and the North. It has just placed on the road four new trains composed of corridor coaches of the latest type, replete with every comfort, artistic in design, and furnished throughout in the most liberal and ornate manner. The first of these trains leaves St. Pancras for Edinburgh at 10.35 am, the afternoon 2.10 express running direct from London to Glasgow. The trains from the North leave Edinburgh at 10.5 am and Glasgow 1.30 pm respectively. Judged from the exterior, the new stock resembles very much the type of carriage which the company are now running on their most important trains. For some time the shops at Derby have been turning out coaches with raised roofs, which give the carriages an imposing look, and provide more air space than was formerly to be obtained in a compartment built on the old plan. The new corridor carriages are built on two different plans. Those intended for dining purposes have the passage through the centre ; in the others the corridor runs down the side. The first-class corridor-carriage is divided into compartments holding four persons, two on each side ; while the third-class is so arranged that

143, *above.* Great Northern Railway Dining car, *circa* 1900. Note the wirework basket racks, and ornate seats in cast iron and plush.

144, *below.* A later design of Midland Railway third class dining car, with electric lighting.

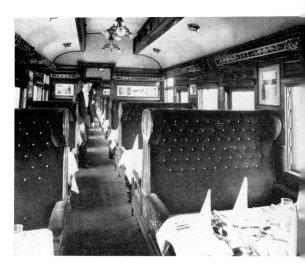

145. Interior of first class saloon, Folkestone Car Train, South Eastern Railway.

six people may be easily accommodated. The interior furnishings for both are all that artistic skill can accomplish. The first is tastefully trimmed with blue cloth with walnut gold lining, and gilded Lincrusta-Walton ceiling. The upholstery of the third is none the less comfortable. The first class dining-coaches have the seats upholstered in red morocco or buffalo hide, and so arranged that they can be pulled forward to make them take the form of a lounge-chair. The new stock has been built in the company's works, under the supervision of Mr. Clayton, ably assisted by Mr. T. P. Osborne.'

This latter description mentions ' raised roofs '; these were of course the clerestory design which came back into vogue, especially on dining cars, in the 'nineties. Gas lighting, in huge pendants (of highly polished brass in many instances) allowed the interior to be better illuminated when a clerestory was used, as the pendant hung low enough for the light to reach all corners of the interior. The clerestory was aesthetically a singularly handsome addition to both interior and exterior of a railway carriage. It somehow bestowed great dignity upon

146, *below.* London & North Western Railway twelve-wheeled dining saloon No. 290. A magnificent example of coachbuilding. The interior, 147, *opposite page,* was elaborate and ornate, and one suspects, also very comfortable.

148, *above.* Midland Railway non-corridor lavatory third, with clerestory roof. The door to the lavatory is between the seats on the right.

149, *below left.* Interior of a first class sleeping car berth, Midland Railway, 1907. The exterior **150,** *below right,* of the same car, 12-wheeled 65 ft. first class car No. 2778.

the whole design, and at its peak, it was a thing of coloured or etched glass and polished brass fittings. The row of small glass panels and ventilators did present a problem to carriage cleaners, however, and this was a factor against the design. On the other hand, the clerestory brought better ventilation and lighting to the carriage interior. Pullman cars had traditionally been associated with clerestory roofs, but in due course it disappeared from these, as well as ordinary carriages.

As in the case of train brakes, the actual design of gangway connection and coupling was the subject of some difference of opinion. The Pullman company introduced some new cars on the Brighton line in 1888, built in America and assembled at Derby. They had enclosed end vestibules (in place of the open verandah of earlier Pullmans) and a flexible gangway of spacious design between the coaches. The Pullman gangway was wide, and it simply butted together with its neighbour. There was a buckeye coupler (automatic) which held the carriages firmly together. The Great Northern Railway adopted this design, using side buffers as well, so that their carriages were capable of being coupled to other stock by the simple expedient of a hinged buckeye coupling, which was dropped to reveal a conventional hook.

The more favoured design of gangway connection was a smaller, lengthy concertina (bellows) type which was joined to its neighbour. Couplings remained the screw-type, first introduced on the Liverpool and Manchester Railway, and long side buffers were fitted. Some 60 years were destined to pass before British Railways finally standardised on the infinitely superior (and safer) Pullman gangway and buckeye coupling.

The American-designed Pullman cars had been highly decorated, ornately furnished vehicles right from the start. They had introduced a new and glittering note to the British railway traveller, with their elaborate gilt work, velvet cloth, walnut panelling and flower-patterned ceilings. They must have startled a good many sober British eyes upon first acquaintance, but there is no doubt of the influence the Pullman car had upon the trend in British carriage design in the last decade of the nineteenth century. The highly-decorated carriage became a matter of some prestige. By 1899/1900 the major railway companies were producing some remarkable feats of artistic coachbuilding, with elaborate interiors filled with choice *Victoriana*. Fine woods such as mahogany and oak were chosen for walls and partitions, with delicate gilt inlay. For upholstery, leather and plush velvet in rich reds, purples, greens and blues might be used, or moquettes in similarly bold colours. Ceilings were usually finished with Lincrusta-Walton relief mouldings which would be painted white, or a pastel shade, and then picked out in gilt. Some very elaborate designs appeared for these ceilings and, particularly when used in conjunction with a clerestory roof, they became a truly magnificent feature. Windows, other than the main side windows, often had elaborately etched designs and some coloured

glass was used. Glass in doors through partitions and in lavatory windows was emblazoned with the company's heraldry, in etched manner. All the small interior fittings—such as luggage rack brackets, light pendants, handles and door knobs—were in highly polished brass with intertwining floral patterns and forms. *Art Nouveau* influence was detectable in some of these smaller fittings, particularly the lamp-brackets and shades, but as a whole *Art Nouveau* did not greatly penetrate the British railway carriage designers' conventions.

From about 1900 onwards there was a general trend towards bogie carriages for main line stock, but it should be pointed out that at that time, these were still a minority; the vastly inferior compartment six-wheeler was still a commonplace of rail travel. The clerestory once again began to lose favour; one reason was the cleaning difficulties it presented, already mentioned, another reason was that it was undoubtedly more expensive to construct. Wood was still the principal material for coachbuilding, but steel was introduced for underframes and headstocks and was gradually used for other items. J. Stone produced a belt-driven dynamo and battery system for lighting carriages with electricity which was to become very widely used in due course, but for the present there was still divided opinion over the relative merits of electricity versus gaslighting and many new carriages were gaslit. Train heating in late Victorian years still depended very much upon foot-warmers and even the sumptuous vehicles just described retained this primitive device. After a number of different experiments a system of carriage heating using steam piped through the carriages from the locomotive was satisfactorily established. In 1905 the Great Western placed in service the largest railway carriages ever built for a British railway, measuring approximately 70ft in length and 9ft 6in in width, with a high elliptical roof. These quickly gained the nickname *Dreadnoughts* (after a contemporary design of battleship). They had end vestibules and a side corridor arrangement that changed from one side of the carriage to the other, via a centre vestibule. The compartments were accessible only from the corridor; they did not have doors opening directly on to the platform. This layout was probably in advance of its time and it must have raised some protests from passengers, because the Great Western afterwards reverted to the door-to-each-compartment layout for its corridor carriages for the next 30 years or so.

Two years after the appearance of the Dreadnoughts, the London and North Western Railway produced a very handsome end vestibuled side corridor design for its ' American ' boat train between Liverpool and

151, *above left.* Interior of North Eastern Railway Dining Car No. 1140, built 1909. This was a first class car, seating 36. Note the *Art Nouveau* influence in the ceiling light fittings and the luggage racks.

152, *above right.* The Great Western Railway *Dreadnought* dining cars were noteworthy for some elaborate furniture, in carved walnut, with Morocco leather upholstery; illustrated is the interior of coach No. 1575, built 1905.

153, *below.* Great Northern Railway Dining Saloon No. 3034, with high elliptical roof.

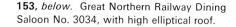

154. First class compartment of one of the special carriages constructed by the L.N.W.R. for their American Boat train, *circa* 1908.

London. Some additional vehicles were also used on the Anglo-Scottish service. These fine vehicles were exceptionally comfortable and vied with the Pullmans used by some other railways. The LNWR had not shown much interest in the Pullman car but these 'American' boat train carriages suggest that they were fully aware of the prestige value of superior design and comfort.

The high elliptical roof found increasing favour because it allowed maximum use of the loading gauge, and gave more headroom to the sides of the carriage. Nigel Gresley employed it on new stock for the Great Northern Railway from 1906, and there were some very high roofed carriages (known as 'Balloon Roofs') on the London Brighton and South Coast Railway. Some railways preferred a lower, flattened elliptical design; only the Midland was still building clerestories by 1914, for main line stock.

The Edwardian era witnessed something of a reaction against the elaborate carriage interiors of late Victorian years. The trend was towards quieter furnishing (with springs replacing buttoned-in seats) and with far less moulding and panelwork. Ceilings were much plainer (emphasised by the high elliptical shape) and the few elaborate touches that did remain, on luggage racks and lamp fittings, etc., seemed rather self-conscious. The passing of the clerestory must be mourned on artistic grounds, for it was replaced by a far less attractive alternative.

By the year 1914 the British main line carriage had reached the dimensions it was to retain for the next 50 years or more, and the pattern was set for lighting, heating and layout.

Finally, we must turn our attention to the suburban and branch line trains; always they seem rather looked upon as the poorer relatives of the main line express.

Suburban carriages up to 1900 were still of basically mid-Victorian design, with four or six wheels, and often closely coupled into sets without corridors or gangways. From this date bogie carriages began to supersede them but new four- and six-wheeled stock remained in service for many more years on some routes. The bogie carriages were of non-corridor compartment type but some had lavatories accessible to compartments within the carriage. The carriages were coupled into sets as had previously been the case, and a logical development took place in 1911 when Gresley produced some articulated suburban train sets, in which adjacent carriages shared a common bogie placed between them. Comfort for suburban travellers remained decidedly stodgy by comparison with the artistic flights of late Victorian main line stock.

A new factor made itself increasingly felt in late Victorian days, causing not a little anxiety to the railways: the development of electric traction. The introduction of electrified City railways (such as the underground City and South London; Waterloo and City, and Central London Railways, and the overhead Liverpool line) had demonstrated the successful replacement of steam power by electricity for intensive suburban working. But this was not all; electric traction had taken to the roads. The electric tram routes spread fanwise from the hearts of our cities; the railway companies were faced with severe competition for

155, *below.* London and North Western Railway, dining saloon No. 6026 of 1914. This was a composite first and third class vehicle.

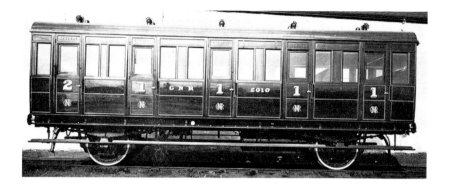

156, *left.* Great Northern Railway non-corridor composite suburban carriage of the early nineteen hundreds. These four-wheelers were designed to operate in close-coupled rakes.

their suburban services. Between 1900 and 1910 the tramcars sapped the railways traffic to an enormous extent, much of it never to be recovered. Trams became a menace which forced the railways to rethink their suburban train service and design. Their answer—Electrification! Already the City railways had been converting to electricity, but partly because of the extreme unpleasantness of steam-worked trains underground. Now the railway companies began to electrify surface lines on suburban routes. The Lancashire and Yorkshire electrified its first line in 1904 and the North Eastern was converting its Tyneside (North) routes the same year. In 1909 the London Brighton and South Coast began electrifying suburban lines in London and, at the end of our

157, *left.* North Eastern Railway Tyneside suburban electric train, with clerestory roofs.

158, *below.* The Midland Railway operated an electric train service between Lancaster Morecambe and Heysham.

159, *above left*. Front end of a Lancashire and Yorkshire Railway electric train of 1904, built to work between Dingle (on the Liverpool Overhead Railway) via Seaforth to Southport. The interior **160**, *above right,* was arranged in saloons. **161**, *below.* Interior of a North Eastern Railway Tyneside electric train showing layout probably influenced by tramcar design ; complete with period commuters ! *Circa* 1904.

162, *left.* Great Northern Railway Steam Rail Car No. 8. Engine and carriage are visually separate units.

present period, the London and North Western Railway had begun work on electrification on its London suburban routes.

Design of the electric suburban trains showed that the railways were willing to learn from the severe lesson of the tramcar. The interiors had a good deal in common with their road-borne counterparts, except on the London Brighton and South Coast Railway, where the conventional compartment-type carriage was retained, although some had an internal side passageway within the carriage (a rather quaint arrangement). The side passageway variety were confined to the South London line because they were somewhat wider than normal LBSCR stock.

These early electric trains, operated as multiple units, were to prove very successful although they did not by any means detract from the success of the tramcar. Another idea for improving the economics and appeal of lightly loaded services, was the steam 'rail-motor'. This consisted of a very small tank engine with a coach body attached to it. Many varieties appeared, and for the record I append a list of those in service in 1913:

163, *top right,* The L.N.W.R. Railmotor, seen at Bicester Station, had the engine unit enclosed within the coachwork. The L.B.S.C.R. example 164, *below,* had an enlarged cab extending almost to the chimney. No. 2 is shown on a South Coast local duty.

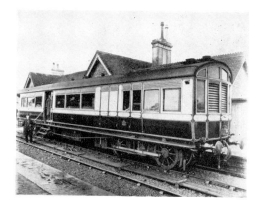

RAIL-MOTOR CARS ON BRITISH RAILWAYS.
(Based upon the Annual Reports for 1913, and other sources of information.)

	Steam	Petrol	Petrol Electric
Alexandra Newport and South Wales ..	1	..	..
Barry	2	..	..
Belfast and County Down	3	..	..
Caledonian	..	1	..
Cardiff	2	..	..
Freshwater Yarmouth and Newport	..	1	..
Furness	1	..	..
Glasgow and South-Western	3	..	..
Great Central	3	..	1
Great Northern	6	..	..
Great Western	99	..	1
Kent and East Sussex	1	..	..
Lancashire and Yorkshire	17	..	..
London and North-Western	7	..	..
London and South-Western	24	..	..
Do. share of joint stock.	2	..	..
London Brighton and South Coast	2	..	..
Do. share of joint stock.	1	..	..
Midland Great Western	..	1	..
North-Eastern	..	5	..
North Staffordshire	3	..	..
Northern Counties Committee	2	..	..
Port Talbot	1	..	..
Rhymney	1	..	..
South-Eastern and Chatham	8	..	..
Taff Vale	16	..	..
	205	8	2

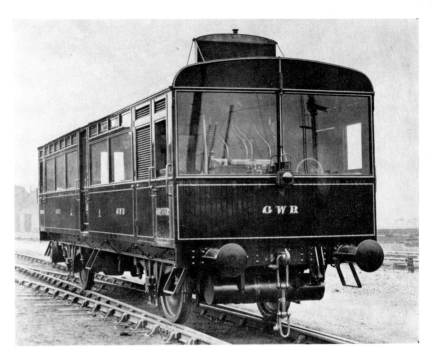

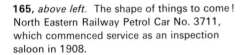

165, *above left.* The shape of things to come! North Eastern Railway Petrol Car No. 3711, which commenced service as an inspection saloon in 1908.

166, *above right.* Great Western Railway Petrol-Electric rail bus, which ran on the Windsor Branch in 1912.

Unfortunately rail-motors were not an unqualified success because of their limited capacity and power. If they built up traffic to the extent that a trailer could be required they were not always powerful enough to haul the extra load. Nevertheless they are an interesting example of Edwardian awareness of growing competition from the roads. The very term 'rail-motor' perhaps chosen unconsciously, reminds us that the motor-car was already on the scene, although as yet something of an expensive novelty. The railways still had a virtual monopoly of passenger business over routes of more than 30 miles or so. They had been brought to harsh reality by the electric tram regarding their suburban services—but no-one could have foreseen the incredible mechanical progress that would be made both on the roads and in the skies during the terrible years of war that lay ahead. But now I anticipate my second volume; that is another story. In August, 1914, the British steam railway reigned supreme, and its passenger carriages presented a civilised means of transport. Very shortly they would be pressed into service to assist in retaining that civilisation. Picnic saloons became hospital trains, with emergency operating theatres. But let us close this chapter with the happier vision of the tremendous progress in carriage design achieved between 1870 and 1914—the golden age of steam railways.

7 Architecture after 1870

By 1870 the greatest years of railway architecture were over, and already the reaction of late Victorian industrial vulgarity was setting-in. Some singularly bleak stations were constructed in the last decades of Queen Victoria's reign, and much of the pioneer enthusiasm which had earlier produced so many classics, was gone forever. The latter-day extensions to earlier buildings were all too often vastly inferior in design. To take Euston for example: each new addition to cope with increased business seemed to assist in turning the place into a rabbit-warren. Where new stations were built, as extensions were opened, a dreary sameness seemed to characterise them.

True, there were some splendid exceptions. There were still a number of great iron roofs to be completed, for example at Darlington (1877), York (1877) and Manchester Central (1880), and on a somewhat smaller scale, the lovely Bath, Green Park (1870).

When York was opened it was the largest station in the world, and the impressive interior, with its great roof curved from end-to-end, remains—in the present writer's humble opinion—the finest example of its kind ever constructed. It represents the climax of the big iron and glass overall roof trainsheds first introduced by Dobson at Newcastle (Chapter Three).

Another magnificent exception to the general dreariness were some of the later bridges. The tragic story of the original Tay Bridge design, by Bouch, is far too well known to need repeating. Its collapse

167, *above.* York station, completed 1877.

168, *below.* The magnificent Forth Bridge, by Fowler and Baker, opened 1890. Photographed by G. F. Heiron in 1955, as a Kings Cross–Aberdeen express was crossing.

during a gale on December 28th, 1879, whilst a train was crossing, was a disaster due to a combination of bad design, bad workmanship and bad maintenance. But it had stood up long enough to prove indispensable; a second Tay Bridge design was commissioned just 19 months after the collapse of the first. The longest viaduct in the world when built (just as Bouch's design had been before it), it was designed by W. H. and Crawford Barlow, and stands adjacent to the stumps of the disastrous first attempt. It is an impressive effort, but undeniably ugly.

Without doubt, the classic of late Victorian railway bridge design is the world-famous Forth Bridge, which even today is an awe-inspiring structure with a truly majestic sense of scale; it is still one of the largest bridges in the world. Design of this masterpiece was the responsibility of Sir John Fowler and Benjamin Baker, in consultation with T. E. Harrison and W. H. Barlow. Baker was taking no chances of a repetition of the Tay Bridge disaster; he conducted a series of experiments in the effects of wind pressures, on the site. The final design, opened to rail

169, *above left.* The cathedral-like structure of the roof, Liverpool Street Station, G.E.R.

170, *above right.* The cast iron spandrels of the station roof at Melton Constable station, incorporating the initials C.N.R. (Central Norfolk Railway).

171, *below right.* The ticket collectors' hut, down side, Westcliff-on-Sea station. A very beautiful example of the fretted valances that were a characteristic of many station roofs.

traffic on March 4th, 1890, by the Prince of Wales, was of cantilever principle.

Mention was made in Chapter Three of the verandahs, which, supported on cast-iron columns or cantilevered out, became a characteristic of the ordinary-sized British railway station. These verandahs were frequently very fine, and a great deal of ingenuity was shown in the design of the wooden valances and cast iron pillars and brackets. The repetitive motifs cut-out by skilled carpenters are one of the most attractive items characterising railway architecture. Many and varied were the designs these men produced, and their pretty silhouette quality lends a great deal of attraction to what could otherwise be a commonplace item. Some were very simple, some possessed intricate repeats; all were quite beautifully executed. On many late Victorian stations these decorative valances are almost the sole redeeming feature.

A blight which settled upon railway architecture during the 'seventies and 'eighties, and from then onwards, was the enamel advertisement which was screwed to all available prominent surfaces— walls, fences, cutting sides, etc.—to catch the eye. Passengers were urged, in coloured enamel, to buy this or that ink, soup, soap, tonic, and suchlike. Some of these signs seem to be indestructible; one still sees them occasionally, used to patch up a shed or fence in a backgarden adjacent to the railway line! They were a manifestation of the increasing spirit of commercialism—how George Stephenson or Brunel would have loathed them. Certainly they would not have been tolerated!

On country stations the platforms were often enlivened by small gardens, or even hanging baskets and tubs of flowers beneath the verandah. Pride in the job was such that these station gardens often became real showpieces, with the station name worked in different coloured blooms or perhaps topiary hedges in a row behind the platform fencing. Of course, life on these stations was often very leisurely and there was plenty of time to attend to such things 'between trains'. There is no doubt that the wayside British station often possessed great character and charm and such touches sadly are missing on present day

172. A selection of decorative effects used for the valances of station roofs and wooden awnings. Drawing by the author.

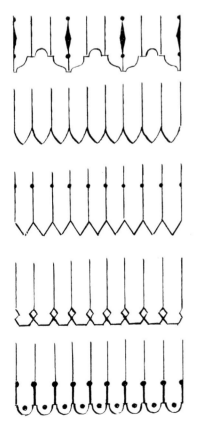
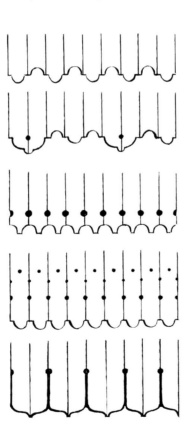
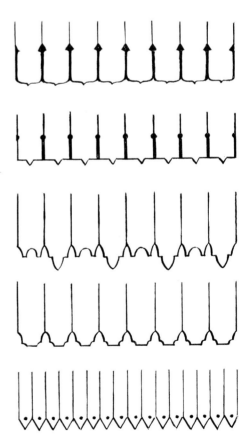

173, *top of page.* Cromford Station, Midland Railway. A compound 4-4-0, No. 1021, thunders through, but the gentleman reading the paper appears not to notice! Note the advertisements affixed to the fences.

174, *above.* Rural station scene; Caythorpe on the Grantham–Lincoln line.

stations; only occasionally can a glimpse of something like it be seen nowadays.

Station hotels, in large cities and towns, were frequently places of some magnitude and importance, and some impressive examples were constructed. In some cases they enhanced the station proper, in others they dominated it even to the extent of hiding the station from view. The Euston hotel, now demolished along with the station, began as two buildings flanking the main entrance to the station (through the Propylæum). In due course the two halves were joined, and as a result the great arch was absurdly hidden from view.

When the Great Central Railway reached London in 1899 it erected a large hotel in Marylebone Road, right in front of the station. The hotel was quite dignified, if not exactly an architectural masterpiece; but the trainshed beyond was a poor, uninspired affair. The great days of railway station building were over. The rebuilt joint Victoria stations of the Brighton and Chatham companies, standing alongside one another, were both poor architectural essays with a general air of decadent classicism.

By 1914 many of the earlier stations had been submerged beneath latter-day additions, or even completely replaced, in order to cope with the greatly changed traffic conditions. There were increasing signs that railway architecture was in the doldrums, basically because the demand for new buildings had dropped almost to nil. Added to this were the effects of constant exposure to soot and industrial grime, becoming increasingly evident to the eye. Nevertheless standards of maintenance and of day-to-day cleanliness were very good. The drastic effects of war were yet to be felt.

8 | Liveries and Decorations

Without doubt, the period 1870–1914 included the finest examples of locomotive and rolling stock liveries. The increasing competition between railway companies, plus a growing awareness of public interest in their activities, made them place great emphasis upon the appearance of their trains. The great junctions and joint stations were the meeting-places for trains of many different companies, and the value of ready identification of *their* trains, as opposed to those of competitors, did not escape them. Even small companies operating purely local services were sufficiently proud to want their own individual livery.

A major junction, such as York or Carlisle, presented a glorious galaxy of colourful liveries, with engines of one company replacing those of another before the train went forward on the next stage of its journey. What fascinating places these were; the Victorian equivalent of today's international airports—but far more exciting to watch!

Space does not permit, nor needs warrant, my listing in detail all the many and beautiful liveries produced during these years; in any case specialised books have been published on the subject. Rather, I would take a few of the classic liveries and leave these to speak for the rest. But first, a word about the general application of liveries to trains.

The basic reason for painting and varnishing a locomotive or carriage was preservation, not decoration. Locomotives had to be proofed against rust and corrosion; carriages against deterioration of woodwork. Beneath the final glossy appearance some very important groundwork was essential, no matter what colour was chosen for the stock to be finished in. An extract from 'The Construction of the Modern Locomotive' by George Hughes, dated 1894, is worth quoting in full:

... The engine is then handed over to the paint shop.

Here it first receives a thorough scouring all over with sandstone, and is afterwards washed down with turpentine, to thoroughly cleanse it from all rust and dirt. It is then given one coat of oil lead colour, which consists of white lead and common black, mixed with boiled linseed oil, turpentine and terebene drier. This coat gives adherence to the stopping and filling, which consists of white lead, Indian copal varnish and gold size. The whole surface of the engine is gone over first, and the worst parts filled up with a thick stopping, using putty knives

175, *top of page.* London & South Western Railway Adams class O2 0-4-4T No. 185, specially named *Alexandra,* and decorated on the occasion of the opening of the Brookwood–Bisley branch on July 12th, 1890. H.R.H. the Princess of Wales (afterwards Queen Alexandra) was in attendance. Drawing by the author.

176, *above.* London & South Western Railway crest on the splasher of an Adams 4-4-0.

and then followed with a thinner stopping worked on with trowels. The rivets are then brushed round with a thinner filling, which softens that put on with trowels, and makes the whole a smooth surface. A cheaper material is mixed with the white lead and used after the first coat of lead colour, when the surfaces are worse than usual and a great quantity of material is required. It is then stained with one coat of vegetable black, mixed with gold size and turpentine, which acts as a guide for the rubbers-down. A smooth surface is then got up by wet rubbing with Schumachersche's Fabrick. Afterwards it receives the first coat of paint, which is a dark lead, mixed in a manner similar to the light lead colour used before filling up. This is followed by a coat of the best drop ivory black, which is mixed with gold size and turpentine, bound with varnish. The third coat consists of the best drop ivory black mixed with varnish, upon which the lining out is done. It is then ready for the varnish, the first two coats being flattened down with pumice powder, horsehair and water, followed by a third coat; best engine copal varnish being used in all cases. The cab is filled up inside in a similar manner to the rest of the engine, and painted with three coats of buff or stone colour, which consists of white lead, Turkey burnt umber, orange chrome, mixed with boiled oil, turpentine and terebene driers. It is then stencilled, lined out, and given two coats of clear varnish. All the motion work, where not bright, and the bufferbeam, receives three coats of vermilion and varnished. Wheels, framing, smoke-box and brake gear receive one coat of drop ivory black and two coats of the best Japan black. The whole operation occupies about three weeks, including one week for the varnish to set, and it is such that it will not be required to be repeated for five years.

In Chapter Five I mentioned the beautiful livery produced by William Stroudley. The basic colour, a warm golden ochre, had the slightest hint of green about it. Even so there is confusion over the description Stroudley used. He called it his 'Improved Engine Green'. Any suggestion that he was colour blind or suffered from defective sight is ludicrous. My own belief is that the name arose quite simply because when Stroudley first applied his new colours to some Highland Railway locomotives he used the current workshop parlance of Inverness, where engines had previously been painted dark green. The term 'engine green' had come to mean the colour used for locomotives; Stroudley *improved* upon it. Another name for it was 'Scotch Green'.

Stroudley brought his new livery to Brighton from Inverness, and ironically Dugald Drummond took it back north of the border when he moved from the Brighton company to take over on the North British Railway. Stroudley's scheme relied upon elaborate 'lining-out' for its rich effect. The ochre was enhanced and enriched by the careful choice of colours used in juxtaposition. Basically the scheme, as shown in the colour plate of *Fenchurch* reproduced on page 108, comprised: main body colour, a rich golden ochre with slightest tendency towards

177, *below left.* Detail of the lining-out and makers' plate on a Fletcher locomotive, North Eastern Railway.

178, *below right.* Lining-out and crest on Lancashire & Yorkshire Railway 2-4-2T No. 1008.

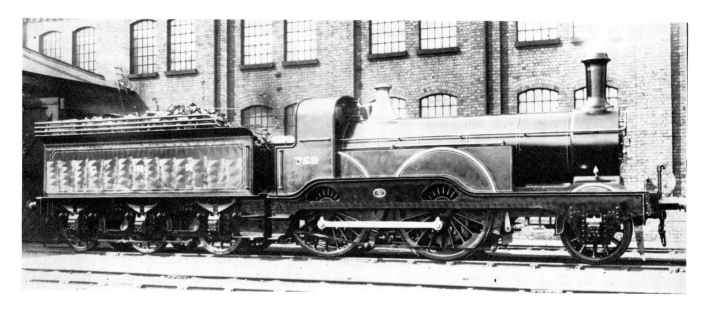

green; next to this a white line, then a black band, then a red line, edged by a panel of dark olive green. Boiler bands were black, with a red line on each side, then a band of olive green with finally a white line next to the ochre. Frames were claret colour, with a black edge with yellow line on the inner side and red line on the outer. Wheels were ochre, with black tyres and olive green axle ends. Locomotive names were in gold-leaf on the ochre, shaded to the left by a graduated emerald green to red on white, and to the right by black. Buffer beams were claret, with a panel of vermilion bordered by a black stripe lined with red and yellow. Coupling rods were often claret coloured; the inside frames, guard irons and leading sand pipes were vermilion. The chimney and smokebox were black; the top of the chimney having a polished copper cap. Cab roofs were lead white, and the tops of tenders were finished with red lead. The numberplate (see later) was brass with a dark blue background. Anyone wishing to see a really authentic contemporary version of Stroudley's magnificent livery is advised to inspect the lovely model of his 0–4–2 *Como*, in the Brighton Museum. Stroudley's goods engines were painted in dark olive green and black. Those fitted with through brakes had a vermilion line on each side of the black line.

Other companies' liveries for their passenger engines were only slightly less elaborate. The Caledonian Railway had a lovely Prussian blue, lined black and white with crimson lake frames. The Great Eastern had quite a different royal blue, with black separated by a vermilion line. Many companies favoured green, ranging from sage green to bright apple green and deep Brunswick green. In each case the associated ' lining-out ' was carefully chosen to enhance the body colour. Reds of differing hues were also employed, ranging from brick reds to deep crimsons and magentas. Black was a most efficient colour for steam locomotives; the Lancashire and Yorkshire and London and North Western both used it, with attractive ' lining-out '. The important point to remember is that the black was beautifully finished and varnished, so that it possessed a richness and a definite warmth, quite opposed to the lack-lustre black engines of the mid-twentieth century.

The wonderful Midland Railway crimson lake livery, introduced by S. W. Johnson, depended upon a painstaking building-up of successive coats of paint and varnish to achieve its glowing warmth of tone. Synthetic modern paints, speedily applied, cannot reproduce the same intensity of colour today.

One could go on, *ad infinitum*, describing the many superb locomotive liveries of the period, but one final example must serve. This was introduced by Henry Wainwright on the South Eastern and Chatham Railway around the turn of the century. It was the last of the truly elaborate liveries. Basically it comprised a Brunswick green body colour,

179. Victorian locomotives were kept spotlessly clean. A typical example of the care lavished upon their finish is G.N.R. 2-4-0 No. 759, seen here. Note the decorative effects worked into the tallow on the tender sides.

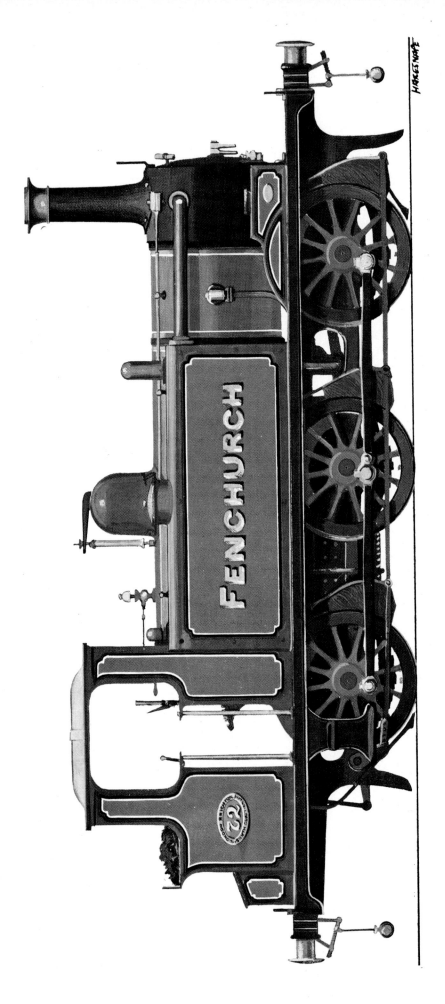

HAKESNAPE

180, *above.* Stroudley's superb golden ochre livery, or 'improved engine green' is shown here applied to one of his diminutive 'TERRIERS' No. 72 *Fenchurch,* built 1872. Original drawing by the author.

181, *lower page.* A selection of pre-grouping carriages in their respective liveries.
Top row, left: Lancashire & Yorkshire Railway brake third of the 1880's. *Top row, right:* South Eastern & Chatham Railway brake third of *circa* 1901. *Second row:* East Coast Joint Stock 55ft. corridor third, built 1896.
Third row: London & South Western Railway

lavatory brake third, built *circa* 1910.
Bottom row: G.W.R. 68ft. 'Dreadnought' corridor composite of 1905. From original drawings prepared by G. M. Kichenside and V. K. Welch.

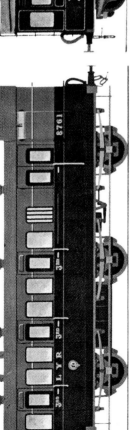
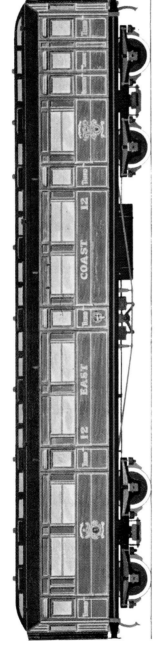
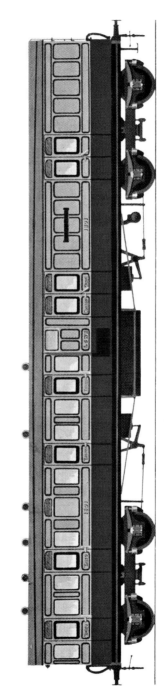
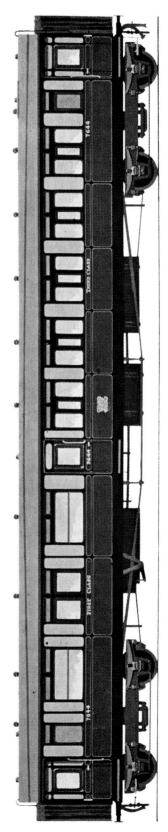

This page:

182, *above.* Coat of arms of East Lancashire Railway, removed from the frontage of Bury Bolton Street station, prior to reconstruction.

183, *below left.* Hull & Holderness Railway coat of arms. **184,** *below right.* Coats of arms of the London & Birmingham Railway on the gates, Euston Station.

Opposite page:

185, *top of page.* Coat of arms, York and North Midland Railway. **186,** *centre.* Coat of arms, North Staffordshire Railway. **187,** *bottom left.* Coat of arms, London, Brighton & South Coast Railway. **188,** *bottom right.* Coat of arms, East Coast Joint Stock.

with a fine yellow line, a broad band of pale sea green, a fine red line and a border of black. The frames were light brown edged with black separated by a red line, with an adjacent yellow line. The chimney cap was polished copper, and the dome cover polished brass. Wainwright's livery was most attractive, but expensive to apply. By 1912 it was modified to reduce the cost; all brasswork and copper was painted over, and the 'lining-out' was simplified. The great days of locomotive liveries were drawing to a close. Stroudley's ochre had already given way to Marsh's umber brown on the Brighton line, and the Highland Railway was painting its engines plain green, totally devoid of lining. Some railways managed to retain their schemes up to the 1914–18 war, but before then the general trend was already towards simplified, less expensive liveries.

Finally, on the subject of locomotive liveries, a word about cleaning. Victorian and Edwardian locomotives positively gleamed and the effects of constant polishing and cleaning greatly enhanced their liveries by producing a rich patina on top of the varnish coats. Engine drivers were responsible for their own engines and there was no shortage of apprentice cleaners at the sheds. A dirty locomotive was unthinkable, it was cleaned outside and in, regularly; below the frames and inside the frames. Metal fittings were kept burnished and oiled to prevent rust, and copper and brass was highly polished. Pride in the job was reflected in the sparkling exterior of even the humblest tank engine, whilst the large main line steam locomotive was a joy to behold.

Carriage liveries were also colourful and varied during this period, with the same careful attention to finish before they left the workshops. Some companies preferred to retain the natural wood finish, preserving it with coats of varnish and enhancing it with 'lining-out'. Others preferred to use a painted scheme, either of one colour overall, or else a two-colour scheme above and below the waist. Panelling was emphasised by 'lining-out' the relief mouldings. It would be impossible to list all the hundred or more carriage liveries in use during this period, so I must content the reader with a description of what was undeniably one of the most popular, the so-called 'chocolate-and-cream' of the Great Western Railway.

As applied during the 1890's this was an elaborate and beautiful livery. The waist panels and lower panels, including underframe, were Windsor brown (also the body ends); above the waist, the panels were creamy-white. The mouldings had a broad black band and a thin brown line on their flat outer surfaces, with gold-leaf on the curved sides. Mouldings of the droplights and quarterlights were varnished natural

wood. Roofs were white, and ironwork was black (other than the brown underframes). The numerals were in gold leaf shaded with black.

A typical feature of practically all carriage liveries during this period was the way the mouldings and panelling of construction were turned into decorative features. Sometimes these ' lining-out ' schemes became so prominent that they detracted attention from a relatively sombre body colour. On some railways the carriages were painted in the same colours as the locomotives, or in colours very similar. On others a definite contrast was achieved; but always with pleasing effect. The standards of taste and craftsmanship exhibited were often quite superb.

Just as in the case of steam locomotive liveries, the cost of applying the elaborate late Victorian schemes to carriages was proving somewhat exorbitant by 1905; despite this many liveries remained unchanged up to the outbreak of the First World War. A good many hearts were broken when, in 1908, Churchward changed the Great Western livery to a chocolate-lake overall scheme, with yellow and black ' lining-out ', and so it remained until 1922.

A feature of railway liveries during the period 1870–1914 was the greatly increased use of identification marks by the various companies. Sometimes this took the form of an elaborate monogram of their initials; sometimes the name was displayed in full (sometimes without the word *railway*) and coats-of-arms were widely used Of the latter, some examples were true heraldry and some were rather dubious; all added an undeniable richness to the scene. The granting of coats-of-arms to railway companies was permissible, as they came under the heading of companies which dealt with services rather than goods.

Many of the railways' heraldic devices were very complicated in origin and meaning, and the present author does not profess the specialised knowledge to expound upon them at great length. On some, the ' arms ' of earlier amalgamated companies were linked together. Often the coats-of-arms of major counties or cities served by the railway were included. Suggestions of speed by means of allusion to Mercury*; by showing a locomotive, or wheels, were also a feature of some. Heraldry certainly lent an air of distinction to the locomotives and carriages, with a very decorative and colourful effect. A few examples are illustrated, and I would rather that these spoke for themselves.

* Mercury—messenger of the gods.

189, *above.* The superb crimson lake livery of the Midland Railway was greatly admired. It certainly suited S. W. Johnson's engines. Illustrated is his 4-2-2 No. 2601 *Princess of Wales,* the largest single to run on a British railway. Drawing by the author.

190, *below left.* Midland Railway Coat of Arms on Compound 4-4-0 No. 1000. The Midland frequently employed the Wyvern as their symbol, even using it in the etched glass window of carriage toilets! 191, *bottom of page.*

192, *below right.* Coat of arms. Great Western Railway.

Typical situations for coats-of-arms, on locomotives, were on driving wheel splashers, cab side sheets or tender sides. Sometimes they were flanked by the name or initials of the company. Particularly attractive were Robinson's Atlantics on the Great Central Railway, where the coat-of-arms appeared no less than three times on each side—one on each driving wheel splasher and one on the tender !

The numbering of locomotives, for record purposes, became a general policy. Gone were the days when locomotive fleets were so small that they could be remembered by individual characteristics, or name alone. Naming was still in some favour, although the tendency now was to name the passenger engines and not the goods types, and on a few railways (such as the Midland) the practice had virtually died out. Both names and numerals presented opportunity for enriching the overall livery by suitable choice of letterforms, and style of application. It was typical of the thoroughness of the Victorian 'Artist Engineers' that these details should receive very close attention.

Polished brass plates were particularly favoured, both for their permanence and attractiveness. They usually took the form of a casting

with raised figures and lettering, with the background painted red, blue or black or left polished. Alternatively the polished brass plate could remain the outer surface, with countersunk lettering filled with black wax, or paint, for contrast. A further, and rather attractive, method was to cut out, or cast, the individual letters and numbers and affix these separately, either directly on to the cabside or boiler sheets, or else to a plate. This last method allowed greater freedom for spacing words, and easier replacement if accidentally damaged.

The actual styles of lettering used were frequently of great character and beauty, and they seemed to 'belong' to the steam age, with their bold shapes and brassy finish. The earliest nameplates were usually lettered with 'serif' letterforms of Egyptian type. (Heavy slab

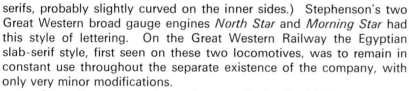

193, *left.* One of the most elaborate Coats of arms belonged to a minor company, the Manchester, South Junction & Altrincham Railway.

194, *above.* Coat of arms, Caledonian Railway.

195, *below.* Garter emblem used on North Eastern Railway passenger coaches.

serifs, probably slightly curved on the inner sides.) Stephenson's two Great Western broad gauge engines *North Star* and *Morning Star* had this style of lettering. On the Great Western Railway the Egyptian slab-serif style, first seen on these two locomotives, was to remain in constant use throughout the separate existence of the company, with only very minor modifications.

Sanserif types were becoming popular by the 1850's, and many railways adopted these for name and numberplates, probably partly because they were easier to draw and cast. One curious tradition was that of Crewe Works on the London and North Western Railway. Nameplates had *sanserif* lettering, countersunk on a brass plate; whereas the numberplates had raised Egyptian slab-serif numerals (incidentally, of more subtle beauty than their Great Western counterparts).

Date and place of construction were sometimes incorporated into either name or numberplate and sometimes cast or engraved upon a separate small brass plate. The practice of casting brass numberplates flourished under the influence of Stroudley and Drummond. Stroudley's numerals were most distinctive. He first introduced them on the Highland Railway (where David Jones continued to use them) and they became a characteristic of the London Brighton and South Coast. The style was a very 'fat' curved serif form, with a most peculiar '7' which was in fact just like a '2' upside-down. Drummond favoured countersunk numerals of sanserif type upon an oval brass plate.

Scarcely less rich in character were the painted version of names and numerals. These would frequently be executed in gold leaf with elaborate shading and countershading. Thus an illusion of the letters standing in relief would be created (very similar to the traditional fairground styles); here again both heavy *serif* and *sanserif* types were used to great effect. Stroudley, already noted above for his beautiful brass numberplates, preferred to have the names of his engines painted on to the golden ochre colour scheme, and so it was with a number of other railways where the Stroudley influence was felt, such as the North British and Highland Railways.

Perhaps the most delightful of all the embellishments of Victorian and Edwardian locomotives were those done by the enginemen and shed staff themselves. These took two forms, one fairly permanent, and one decidedly to the contrary. The permanent form included burnished decorative shapes on smokebox doors and buffers, or polished rivet heads

196, *top left.* Numberplate, Lancashire & Yorkshire Railway 2-4-2T No. 1008. 197, *above.* Numberplate, North Eastern Railway 4-4-0 No. 1621. 198, *top right.* Numberplate, London, Brighton & South Coast Railway 0-4-2 No. 214. 199, *right.* Numberplate Fletcher locomotive No. 910, North Eastern Railway. 200, *below.* Drawing of number-plate, London & North Western Railway.

201, *top left.* Worksplate, North Eastern Railway.

202, *centre left.* Midland Railway worksplate, on 4-4-0 No. 1000. 203, *above.* Worksplate on London, Brighton & South Coast Railway 0-6-0T 'Boxhill'. 204, *below.* Dubs & Co. worksplate of 1874.

205, *right.* Nameplate of North Eastern Railway locomotive *Aerolite*.

206, *below left.* Great Western Railway nameplates were characterised by a distinctive Egyptian slab-serif letterform from the earliest days. Illustrated are four Broad gauge locomotive nameplates.

207, *below right.* Nameplate of G.W.R. 4-4-0 *City of Truro*; note the sans-serif letterform used for the word 'of'. **208**, *bottom of page.* Blue-print of Great Western Railway alphabet for locomotive nameplates. Shown reduced from full size. Although dated 1937, it is almost certainly a tracing of a much earlier drawing.

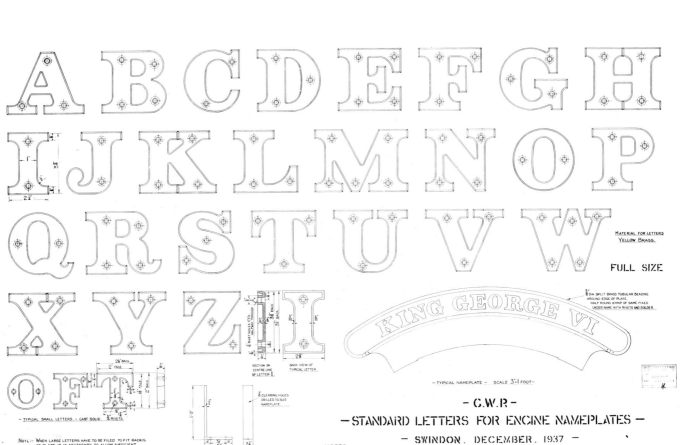

or other constructional details. Painstaking scraping away of layers of paint was a prerequisite to these decorations. Once the bare metal was exposed it was burnished until it shone bright. Many Scottish locomotives had thistles or stars burnished upon the smokebox doors, according to the individual fancy of the enginemen. (Much to the author's delight, he can recall this tradition still flourishing in some areas of Scotland in the mid-1950's.) Brass filigree was also widely applied.

The other form of embellishment was akin to the idea of dressing-up horses for a ceremonial parade. A true sense of occasion seems to have prevailed in railway circles during this period. A funeral, Coronation, Diamond Jubilee or other royal event was the excuse for elaborate preparations. Garlands of everlasting flowers were arranged along boiler sides, or placed in wickerwork baskets. Portrait busts were mounted upon bufferbeams, along with coats-of-arms and various royal devices. The whole engine was cleaned and polished until it shone like a new coin, and to crown it all the coal was whitewashed!

No less favoured were visiting foreign princes; politicians; famous generals, or even soldiers returning from the Crimea. Whilst the annual Stationmasters' and Inspectors' excursion to the sea-side was an opportunity seized to garland an engine in truly festive spirit. No carthorse ever looked as gay as these 'iron horses'.

Picture if you would St. Pancras Station on a dull morning. All about you are the handsome crimson lake trains of the Midland Railway, with important destinations. What startled eyes must have been raised from their newspapers, as an engine steamed slowly into view to couple on to that insignificant train of carriages belonging to the London Tilbury and Southend Railway. The headboard read as usual 'Southend', and it was one of the company's typical 4–4–2T locomotives, No. 80 *Thundersley*. But what a fantastic spectacle it was; for this was the time of Coronation of King George V.

A photograph of *Thundersley*, reproduced on page 119, defies any further description on my part. *Of course* the Midland Railway

209. Great North of Scotland Railway nameplate on 4-4-0 *Gordon Highlander,* using a typical sans-serif style.

210, *below.* Decorated front of North British Railway 'Atlantic', *Highland Chief.* Such decoration was usually done by the engine driver in his spare time, by burnishing the steel parts to a bright finish or adding brass filigree.

frowned upon such frivolities! Its own royal engine was distinguished purely by a cipher on the cabside (see illustration on page 120).

Finally, a trivial thought. I have often wondered how much of the decoration was lost *en route.* The spectacle of *Thundersley* leaning into the curves as she sped alongside the Thames estuary towards Westcliff and Southend, with garlands of flowers flapping wildly in the slipstream and busts of Their Majesties jogging merrily to the beat of the exhaust, leaves me happily speculative!

Opposite page: **211,** *top.* G.W.R. locomotive *Lord of the Isles,* decorated June 24th, 1873, for soldiers returning from the Crimean war. **212,** *bottom.* Stroudley 0-4-2 No. 188 *Allen Sarle,* at Eastbourne on an annual excursion of Station Masters and Inspectors, from Victoria, L.B.S.C.R. **This page:** **213,** *above.* L.T. & S.R. 4-4-2T No. 80 *Thundersley* decorated for the Coronation of King George V. **214,** *below.* Garlands for London, Brighton & South Coast Railway Billinton 4-4-0 No. 54 *Empress.*

215, *top of page.* The Midland Railway Royal engine, with cipher on cabside. It was No. 502, a standard inside cylinder 4-4-0.

216, *above left.* Drummond 4-4-0 No. 729, London & South Western Railway, at Nine Elms.

217, *above right.* L.B.S.C.R. Marsh 'Atlantic' No. 39, named *La France* and decorated with red, white and blue ribbons, to work a special train conveying the French President from Portsmouth Docks to London.

218, *above left.* Decorated train lamps used for Royal Journeys in the nineteenth century.

219, *right.* Decorated fitments from Royal trains of the G.W.R. and L.B.S.C.R.

9 | Ephemera, Notices and Uniforms

We have already seen in Chapter Four how the early railway printed matter was left very much to the instinctive taste of the individual printer, with remarkably happy results. In the 1870's and 1880's this remained much the same situation although greater standardisation of typefaces became apparent. Printing upon coloured papers was increasingly used for excursion handbills to attract attention to these items; whilst posters were often in two or more coloured inks, but still basically all-lettering designs.

The development of colour printing for pictorial reproduction (particularly the chromo-lithographic process) offered new scope for publicity. Pictorial posters could be produced in attractive quantities for widespread display, and this was a feature of the railway publicity from Edwardian days, with many famous contemporary artists being employed to produce specially commissioned pictures. The two Midland Railway posters reproduced on page 123 clearly show the change that took place.

As mentioned in the chapter on architecture (Chapter Seven), the advertisement hoarding became a typical feature of railway stations from late Victorian years onwards. Enamel signs were coming into use, but for the more ephemeral publicity the printed poster remained supreme. Another feature was the large hand-painted poster, advertising special excursions (produced in insufficient numbers to warrant the cost of printing) displayed outside large stations. Railway companies advertised their services widely in these highly competitive days, and it was commonplace to find their posters on stations hundreds of miles from their own routes. Thus the Great North of Scotland Railway might well advertise its services in Cornwall; and so on, for these were the days of ' through carriages '.

Printed matter, by nature of its ready production, always tends to follow most readily the current trend in artistic taste. By way of contrast, a more sober approach characterises the applied letterforms of cast-metal signs and notices. The railways produced many types of warning signs and other notices in heavy cast-iron, because of their vulnerability to vandalism or accidental damage. Mileposts and gradient posts are other instances where a high degree of permanence was considered desirable. In fact many of these signs have proved very permanent indeed, and it is not uncommon to come across them in use today. Countless examples have become the treasured possessions of railway enthusiasts or museums. An interesting sidelight is that those signs which were produced in enamels, rather than cast-iron, have suffered far more from the effects of small boys with stones, over the years. One feature, against the favour of cast-iron, is that it is impossible to alter the wording. Hence in 1967 there are still numerous signs bearing the names of railway companies that ceased to exist nearly half-a-century ago. The usual expedient is to paint-out the name and pretend it's not there!

Station names were often built up from cast-iron letters screwed to wooden boards, and small versions of these might be found on seat

220. Poster of 1879, Great Western Railway, printed in Bristol.

London, Brighton and South Coast Railway.

NOTICE.

On and after the 1st October next

THE NAME OF

CATERHAM JUNCTION

STATION

WILL BE

ALTERED TO

PURLEY.

(By Order)   A. SARLE, Secretary & General Manager.

JULY 2nd, 1888.

500)

Waterlow and Sons Limited, Printers, London Wall, London.

221, *top left.* Handbill, 1886. London & North Western Railway.

222, *lower left.* North Eastern Railway poster of 1870.

223, *top right.* Poster of 1888, London, Brighton & South Coast Railway.

backs, on the platform. Some railways favoured painted name signs, but these required greater upkeep. Gas lamps often had the station name in the glass, perhaps reversed out of a deep blue, so that the light shone through the name at night. In Edwardian years the Great Western Railway produced some very elaborate *art nouveau* lettering for the name signs outside stations, in metal, affixed to the frontage. A feature of most direction signs was the use of cast-iron ' pointing ' fingers, or hands, to show the direction to be taken, rather than the arrows favoured today.

Uniform design became very important by the 1870's, as stations grew larger and services more frequent. It was essential for the passengers to be able to identify the appropriate staff, whilst the staff themselves now numbered so many that identification of seniority of rank or grade became imperative. Different styles of headgear and dress identified the various grades, with the top-hat remaining the status-symbol of superior officials. The porter was a very active participant in the railway travel scene of those days; for families were large and luggage was heavy. Much careful shepherding and loading of parents and children, plus trunks and hampers, promised good rewards. The porters' dress, complete with velveteen or corduroy trousers and waistcoat, ideally served him.

The railway guard had become a very dignified figure by the 1850's (see Chapter Four) and he remained so throughout our period. The LNWR guard illustrated on page 126 should be compared with the dapper character illustrated on page 58. Could they in fact be one and

224, *top left.* Midland Railway poster of 1903, printed in two colours.

225, *top right.* The pictorial poster was well established by 1913, when this design was produced by Graham Phillips for the South Eastern & Chatham Railway.

226, *left.* Pictorial poster depicting St. Pancras Station, Midland Railway. Painting by Fred Taylor.

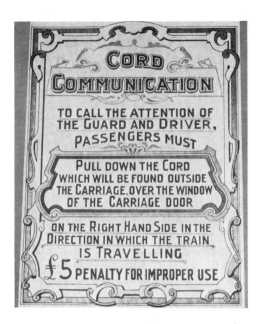

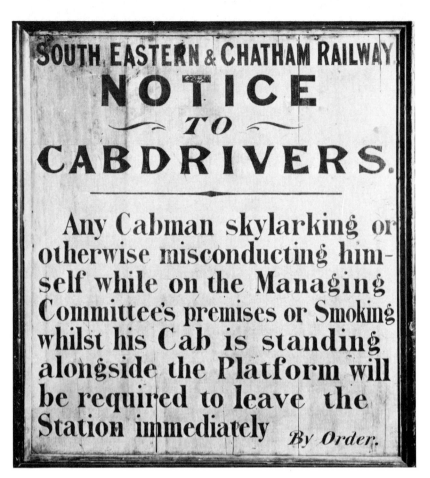

227, *above left.* When in peril or distress, read the notice and follow the instructions carefully! Great Northern Railway carriage notice.

228, *above right.* Painted notice, S.E.C.R.

229, *below left.* Cast iron notice of 1899, London, Brighton & South Coast Railway.

230, *below right.* A very neat cast iron notice of 1896, Great Northern Railway, still in use in the 1960's.

the same? It is quite feasible. Certainly the style of uniform had but little changed over the intervening 50 years or so.

Finally, the engine driver. I have not illustrated him separately in this chapter, as several examples of typical driver's dress are to be found elsewhere in this volume. He remained, throughout the period, in clothing ideally suited to his duties, with very little decorative consideration except possibly a cap-badge. But what an impressive figure he was (the equivalent of any racing driver, airline pilot or even astronaut, today), and the combination of a hot steam locomotive and sweaty coal dust covered driver and fireman at the end of a long journey, scarcely required the frills of a uniform to add romance—it was there in plenty, as every small boy knew!

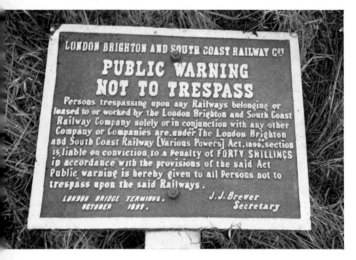

231, *above left.* Rhymney Railway notice.

232, *top right.* Great Western and Great Central Joint Committee notice.

233, *lower right.* Lancashire Derbyshire and East Coast Railway notice.

234, *below.* L.B.S.C.R. staff, 1881. Left to right : Ticket collector ; Ticket inspector ; Station superintendent, Station inspector, Guard and Policeman.

BROCKENHURST, CHANGE FOR LYMINGTON.

235, *above.* Staff at Brockenhurst station, London & South Western Railway, 1900.

236, *below left,* London & North Western Railway guard. (Compare with plate 82).

237, *below right.* Midland Railway Guards.

238, *above.* Porters on the South Eastern Railway, with typical close-coupled suburban carriages. The gentleman peering intently through the window is believed to be the photographer.

239, *left.* A facility for passengers which was probably greatly appreciated. Euston, 1905.

Index

Illustrations

continued overleaf

Illustrations—*continued*